Jerky Everything

Foolproof and Flavorful Recipes
for Beef, Pork, Poultry, Game, Fish,
Fruit, and Even Vegetables

PAMELA
BRAUN

COUNTRY MAN KNOW HOW

The Countryman Press
A division of W. W. Norton & Company, Inc.
500 Fifth Avenue, New York, NY 10110
www.wwnorton.com

For information about special discounts for
bulk purchases, please contact W. W. Norton Special Sales
at specialsales@wwnorton.com or 800-233-4830

Printed in the United States of America

Jerky Everything
ISBN 978-1-58157-271-1

10 9 8 7 6 5 4 3 2 1

Jerky Everything

DEDICATION

For CB and RB for teaching me that simple is better
and everything is easier with thumbs.

CONTENTS

I didn't grow up in a house where jerky was around. As a teenager I tried it, once, and promptly spit it out. The hard as a rock and ridiculously chewy texture combined with some kind of flavoring that tasted like I was chewing on a solid block of Lawry's Seasoning Salt was what ended it for me. Fast-forward a few years—okay, decades—and my love for great cuts of meat combined with my near obsession with a device called a dehydrator allowed me to realize that jerky could not only taste delicious, but is a healthy snack, and ridiculously easy and fairly inexpensive to make. Plus, it's a great way to make friends. More on that later.

I've done a great deal of traveling and have found the foods, flavors, and cooking techniques from around the world have a great influence on the cooking that I do and the recipes I create for clients and my food blog www.MyMansBelly.com. My travels have given me the opportunity to try jerky from many different cultures and countries. Things like *Springbok, kudu,* and plain ol' beef *biltong* in South Africa (I really like the *kudu* jerky). I've had *bakkwa,* or *rougan,* in China and Singapore. In Australia I've eaten jerky that comes from cows, kangaroo, emu, and crocodile. And of course, I've enjoyed lots of various flavors and types of jerky found here in the United States.

With this book, I want to take you on a culinary tour of the world through jerky. Really, this stuff isn't just something to pack away in your emergency kit, for manly men of the bush, extreme weight lifters and bodybuilders, Paleo diet martyrs, or for people who like chewing on pieces of shoe leather. It's a healthy and flavorful snack that's easy to make, easy to eat, and easy to take with you for your busy day.

Creating the recipes for this book has been an adventure. I've met farmers and ranchers through my meat and seasonings research who have schooled me on the finer points of their respective ingredients. My recipe testers and tasters have been beyond enthu-

siastic. I've got sheriff's departments, hockey teams, programmers, co-workers (my husband has made so many new friends), and neighbors that have all been a *huge* part of making sure that these recipes have the taste and flavors to make them a hit at your house. Oh, and if you want to make some new pals, just ask people whether they'd like to have some jerky ... they'll practically hug you just for asking them.

The last time I was at the forefront of a trend, was when I picked out our new house color and then proceeded to see it popping up everywhere. Truth is, it seems that I'm always a half a step behind when it comes to the "cool" things. Take for instance, cake balls. They'd been out for a couple of years already when I finally decided to make them ... and when I did, I shaped them into mice, not balls. It's like my subconscious isn't really sure the trend is going to stick.

Well, now it's my turn to finally be cool (hey, let me have my moment). You've probably seen, or heard, the term *charcuterie* being thrown around as if it's some new cultish religion (for some people, it kinda is). Even though charcuterie sounds like a really fancy term (it is French after all), all it really means is the preservation of meats. Things like bacon, ham, sausage, terrines, galantines, pâtés, confit, and of course ... jerky all fall into this category of charcuterie.

Having never really been a fan of jerky in my youth, one day I asked my husband, Craig, whether he liked the stuff. I know our dog likes it, but I really didn't think I'd get much feedback on it if I made a batch and fed it all to her (although I do make her homemade chicken jerky ... yes, my dog is S-P-O-I-L-E-D). Craig just kind of rolled his eyes and shrugged his shoulders, which in his world is translates to "Sure, I like jerky." So I decided that I would try something new and make homemade beef jerky.

That was three years and hundreds of batches of jerky ago. If I stopped making it now, I'm pretty sure my loyalty and devotion to my husband would be called into question.

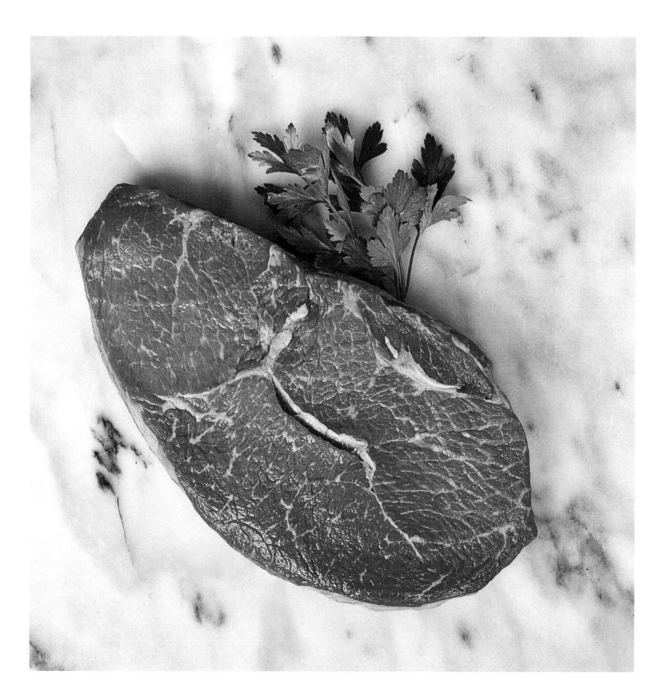

CHAPTER 1

DIY Jerky

Old jerky is bad, just bad. I'm talking about *old school* jerky, the kind that our forefathers (let's face it, the men may have started it ... but it was the women who actually ended up making it) gnawed on. It was created as something to help with survival as people made their way out west or went about their workday out in the fields and riding the range, so flavor wasn't really much of a must-have when the process of jerky making was undertaken.

Fast-forward to a time when dried meat wasn't a necessity to keep us alive, but more something to chew on to keep the hunger pangs at bay and to keep us from losing our mind to boredom while cruising across the country via a four-wheeled horse. Again, flavor was not of utmost importance, but the meat was expected to be at least a step above the flavor of the rubber wheels taking us to our destination. The Egyptians took the time and effort to chisel the virtues of dried meat into stone walls, between the portraits of their beloved cats and ankhs. Seafarers pickled strips of meat, packed them in barrels, and nibbled on the strips as they crossed the vast oceans (and now you know why they were so aggressive ... all that meat consumption can bind a pirate up). African folklore has herders placing strips of meat under their horses' saddles to help tenderize the meat, It is said that the sweat of the horse gave the meat the flavor it needed. (If it was so good, I'm wondering where that sweat spice blend is in today's supermarket.)

From seafarers to cowboys, jerky has been a source of sustenance for centuries—a simple food source created out of the necessity for explorers to

eat and a way to safely preserve food in the days prior to refrigeration.

While the consumption of jerky is the same no matter where or how it is made (open mouth, insert jerky, and chew), it's the making of jerky that has varied by who was making it and where it was being made.

When the Europeans arrived in the New World, they discovered Native Americans making pemmican, which consisted of ground meat mixed with fat and dried berries (usually blueberries and/or cranberries).

The Dutch had their own version of jerky, which they called *tassal*. Not much has been written about *tassal*, and its recipes, beyond the fact that it was some pretty pungent stuff and was the basis for the South African jerky known as *biltong*. *Biltong* is a Dutch word that literally means "strip of ass," and it closely resembles the North American jerky (slab or strip form). The *biltong* strips are thicker than what we're used to in the United States and there is an additional curing agent, also not found in North American jerky recipes: vinegar. For the record, *biltong* is made from the same lean cuts of meat that we use to make jerky . . . not pieces of ass.

Wondering how the word *jerky* came about? *Ch'arki*, an Incan word meaning "dried meat," is where the term comes from.

Today's jerky is being enjoyed by far more people than rugged explorers, cowboys, and truck drivers. Busy executives, health nuts (especially those following the Paleo way of eating), bar patrons, and arbiters of good taste are all enjoying the flavors of jerky. Today's jerky goes well beyond sticks of beef or venison, too. If you can dry it, it seems you can jerky it: poultry, pork, bison, lamb, ostrich, alligator, salmon, tuna, tofu (yes, really), and vegetables are all available for your noshing pleasure. Combine these with the flavorings of the world (through the various spices now available in virtually every supermarket) and you've got the makings of the newest gourmet treat.

Oh, and if you think jerky only comes in ground, strip or slab form, guess again. There is also a little thing called meat floss, a.k.a. jerky chew. While this isn't anything your dentist is going to recommend as a tool for cleaning your teeth, you'll probably find that some has worked its way between your teeth anyway. Meat floss is pretty much what it sounds like—dried and shredded meat. I wouldn't say that it looks or eats like meat cotton candy, more like meat chewing tobacco . . . minus the tobacco.

If you're asking yourself why you should make your own jerky, when there are so many good jerkies out there, then you've never had homemade jerky. Sure, buying jerky is a bit easier (only a bit), but do you know what's in it? Do you like the limited . . . cough . . . teriyaki . . . flavors that are available? Is it too salty? Too expensive? Making your own jerky remedies *all* of these problems.

Can you pronounce all of the ingredients in that package of jerky you bought at the store? If you can, great. Do you know what those ingredients are? Most of the really weird-sounding/looking words are preservatives that give the jerky its shelf life. While making your own jerky won't allow it to have a six- to twelve-month shelf life, you will actually know each

and every ingredient that goes into it. And how about the meat itself? My guess is that your package of jerky, the one that you bought at the store, just lists "beef" for the meat ingredient (presuming it's beef jerky you bought). What cut of "beef" did they use to make it? When you make it yourself, you can choose your own cut of meat from whatever source you like to buy your meat from. I guess what I'm getting at here is better ingredients, better-tasting product, better for you.

One of the best things about making jerky at home is that you can use the flavors that you like. Like curry? Make a curry jerky. Like Cheddar cheese and beer? Make Cheddar ale jerky. The flavor combinations are virtually endless.

How about the salt content? While no one on a salt restricted diet should be eating jerky (salt is one of the main preservatives of the meat), you can greatly reduce the amount of salt when you make your own jerky. You can do this because you are controlling the ingredients, but you're also making more manageable quantities so you don't need the jerky to have such a long shelf life. And if you do need it to hang around a while longer, you can keep it in the refrigerator or pop it into the freezer for even longer storage.

Let's take a look at that cost issue. Store-bought jerky is expensive. A bag of regular ol' jerky (not the gourmet stuff) that you can buy at the drugstore costs almost $2 per ounce. That's $32 per pound . . . even filet mignon isn't $32 per pound at the grocery store. Making your own jerky out of even the most prime cuts of meat is going to save you a lot of money.

So, as you can see, there are lots of benefits of making your own jerky.

The Subject Being Jerkied

SELECT YOUR SUBJECT

You can turn many things into jerky: beef, turkey, pork, emu, alligator, bison, buffalo, wild boar, yak, kudu, tofu, mushrooms, fruit, and the list goes on and on. You can pretty much turn any meat, and some non-meats, into a delicious piece of jerky.

Regardless of what meats you intend to turn into jerky, make sure that you select the leanest cuts you can find. That means cuts of meat that you usually don't want to buy because they often come out dry and tasteless when you cook them under normal circumstances. Those are *the best* cuts for making jerky. I find anything ending in loin, round, or broil is going to give the best results. For poultry, it's going to be the breast meat; and for fish, it will be fillet or steak. You're going to flavor these cuts with delicious marinade, and being lean, they're going to dry really well and have a longer storage life because there isn't any fat on them to go rancid.

Don't be afraid to ask your butcher, or the men/women behind the meat counter, to slice your beef or pork for you. If they're not busy, a lot of times they will. There's not an extra charge for this and it will save you a whole lot of time if you can get your meat pre-sliced. I do it all the time.

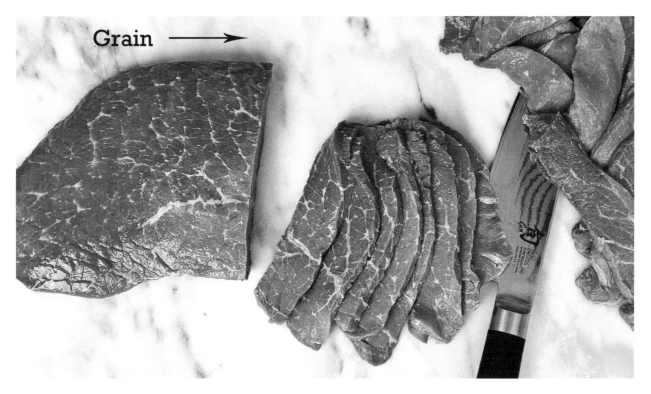

Grain ⟶

Because jerky is dried, and most of the moisture has been removed, the flavors of the meat or vegetable and the marinade are highly concentrated. That means that you should use the best ingredients you can afford. If you use low-quality ingredients, your jerky won't taste as good as it can. I'm not saying that you need to buy prime beef to make your jerky. What I'm saying is that if you know a particular store sells meat that always seems to taste great, buy your jerky meat there.

PREPARE YOUR SUBJECT

To prepare the meats for drying, you need to remove as much fat as possible. Fat is bad for jerky because it doesn't dry out properly and turns rancid quickly.

You also should remove any silver skin that might be on your meat. Silver skin is that tough membrane that you sometimes find on red meat or pork, which looks silvery. Just slip your knife through the sides of the skin and pull your knife along the meat to remove it. This membrane makes it hard to cut your slices and when dried becomes extremely chewy and doesn't add any flavor. Once the fat and silver skin are removed, it's time to cut the meat. You need to decide whether you want strip or slab jerky. You also need to decide whether you want your jerky to be tender (cut across the grain of the meat) or chewy (cut with the grain of the meat.)

Another way that you can prepare your jerky is to

trim the meat of any fat, and silver skin, and marinate it whole, overnight, then cut it into strips and marinate it for a couple more hours before drying. Marinating like this allows more of the meat flavor to shine through the marinade. When you cut the meat into strips and soak them in the marinade, the marinade has a much more pronounced flavor. Either way, your jerky will taste great.

Create Your Marinade

Sure, technically you could just sprinkle a little salt and pepper on the meat and dry away. You could definitely make jerky that way and the salt and pepper would add a nice little bit of flavor to the meat. But why waste all that perfectly good meat by not using it as a premium flavor delivery service for your taste buds?

I've created a lot of different types of marinades, dry rubs, and pastes in this book (which I tend to refer to collectively as a marinade), enough recipes to keep you busy for a while anyway. But making a marinade isn't really all that hard. You can, and should, invent some of your own. Wouldn't it be kind of cool to give out batches of jerky that you created at the holidays?

I like to mix up flavors that taste good to me. Even a restaurant dish that I've had before, I'll break down into its individual flavors and turn into a jerky (see the recipes for Rogan Josh, Orange Beef, and Philly Cheesesteak, for examples).

When you start out creating your own marinade, a good rule of thumb is two parts salt to one part seasoning, either sweet or savory or both. Of course this ratio isn't written in stone, but if you're trying to create your own marinade, this is a good ratio to keep in mind.

When you select your seasonings, think about what flavors go best with the type of meat you'll be drying. Of course you could always go the store-bought marinade/seasoning route, but what fun is that? You've got to spice it up a little bit. Just make sure that you taste your seasoning *before* you put the meat into it. Remember that all those flavors are going to be concentrated. Does it need more salt? Does it need to be sweeter? Is it too strong and need to be diluted it with a little water? Always taste before you marinate!

Substitutions

Many of these marinade recipes are interchangeable with pretty much any of the proteins. It's possible that you may find some of the beef marinades have too strong a flavor on the fish or turkey. Also, I wouldn't use on the beef any of the potato chip–like flavors used on the turkey. These were specially formulated for turkey.

While these recipes are all written for small-batch jerky, they can easily be doubled or tripled for larger batches. One thing to remember when doubling or tripling a recipe containing hot peppers is to keep the number of hot peppers the same as in the original recipe, then taste it to see how many more you should add. The flavor that hot peppers add isn't necessarily a 1:1 ratio.

Those who are forgoing gluten can swap in tamari for soy sauce in any of these recipes. Those who

are followers of Paleo eating can swap out the soy sauce for coconut aminos, but you'll need to add 2 to 3 teaspoons of kosher salt (it depends how much salt flavor you like) for every ¼ cup of coconut aminos that you add. Because coconut aminos have a lot less sodium in them than soy sauce does and the sodium is needed for flavor and preservation of the jerky you need to add back some salt to the recipe. To make the vegetarian recipes vegan, you can substitute tamari for Worcestershire sauce in the recipes. These swaps will change the flavors so slightly that no one will really notice a difference.

How to Dry Jerky

THE EQUIPMENT

There are a few ways that you can dry meat to make jerky. You can use a smoker, an oven, a dehydrator, the good ol' sun, or a roaring fire. Whichever way you

choose to make jerky is up to you and your surroundings. For the purposes of this book, I'm not going to get into making jerky in a smoker (because not many people have access to one) and I'm not going to go through the process of making jerky in the great outdoors, as by this method the healthfulness and quality of the end product are pretty unpredictable. Using the sun to make jerky is how our forefathers did it . . . and they had a life expectancy of thirty to forty years. Considering our natural environments are generally not conducive to making dried meat, I'll stick to discussing the jerky making process using the oven or an electric dehydrator.

MAKING JERKY IN THE OVEN

You can use gas, electric, or convection ovens to make jerky. A couple of issues to consider when making jerky in the oven is that most ovens don't go lower than 200°F (which is pretty hot for making jerky) and there isn't great air circulation around the meat in a regular gas or electric oven (convection ovens do circulate air, however). Jerky made in an oven can be tougher and can taste more "cooked" than dehydrated.

To help get more air around the meat, there are a couple of things that you can do. First, you can stick a wooden spoon handle in the door opening to keep it ajar during the cooking process. You can also place a cooling rack in a sided baking sheet and lay the meat strips on top of the cooling rack. Alternatively, you can also skewer the meat strips with a toothpick or shish kebab stick and hang

the meat strips between the grates of your oven rack. Just place a baking sheet underneath the meat strips to catch any drips. Also, try to set your oven temperature to 165°F. (But you may be stuck with the 200°F.) The drying time tends to be a bit shorter in the oven than in an electric dehydrator, due to the greater heat. Depending on the quantity and thickness of the meat you're drying, the drying time will be between 4 and 24 hours. If using the oven to make your jerky, you'll want to start checking on it after 2½ hours.

While convection ovens definitely circulate the air (no wooden stick in the door), they also cook faster. If you use a convection oven to make your jerky, expect to do a bit of experimentation to find that jerky-making sweet spot. Start checking on the jerky after 90 minutes.

MAKING JERKY IN AN ELECTRIC DEHYDRATOR

I much prefer making my jerky in the dehydrator. I can get the temperature I want, air circulates easily, it only takes a few hours, and I don't need to tend to it while it's working. Plus, it's easy to clean up the dehydrator and its trays.

There are a few different styles of dehydrators but they basically come in two shapes: round or square/rectangular. Either shape works fine. It's important to understand how your dehydrator circulates air. Some do a great job of circulating the drying air around all of your jerky and some don't, so you may need to switch the trays around to help everything dry at an even pace.

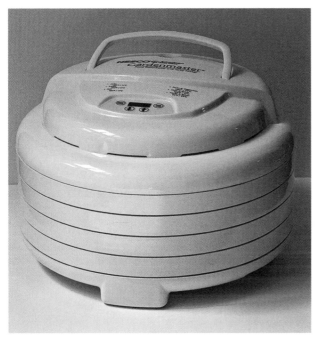 

Jerky needs to be arranged in a single layer on the drying racks and it's best to leave a bit of room between the pieces. This just allows more air to circulate and for your jerky to dry faster.

Typical drying times are listed for each recipe. If no temperature is listed, set your dehydrator to 165°F.

For regular meat, fish, or vegetable jerky, you can use the standard dehydrator trays. For such things as fruit rollups or the liver dog treats, you're going to want to use the solid fruit roll trays. These are nonstick and allow you to dry and remove things easily. You can also use the nonstick mesh sheets on top of the dehydrator trays if you've got a jerky that seems particularly sticky or the pieces are small.

(Remember, as things dry they shrink and could fall through the trays if they're too small.)

While I'm on the topic of dehydrator accessories, I should mention that several dehydrators now also come standard with a jerky extruder. This tool is like a cake frosting gun for ground meat jerky. It can make the process of making ground meat jerky strips easier for you.

It's always a good idea to make sure that your dehydrator is holding a steady, and acceptable, temperature. Sure, the dial on top gives you a number, but you'll still want to check the accuracy. You can pick up a small oven thermometer at your local grocery store. Just pop it onto one of the trays and turn

your dehydrator on, with meat in it, and check the temperature. It should be holding between 160° to 165°F (however, you will soon see that if it's holding at a lower temperature, you may still be in the clear).

Drying Time

Whether you choose to dry your jerky in the oven or in an electric dehydrator, the drying process remains the same.

The meats are all arranged in a single layer with some space between them, air is circulating, and the temperature needs to be a minimum of 145°F, with 165°F the ideal temperature setting for drying.

The time it takes to actually dry the jerky is going to vary, depending on several things. What is the drying temperature? What is being dried? How big/thick are the pieces being dried? How wet are the pieces being dried? How much is being dried? The actual drying time could vary from 4 to 24 hours. Given the batch sizes that you'll find in this book, your drying time will usually fall within the 4- to 6-hour drying time range. Where there is a known exception to that, I have noted it in the recipe itself.

HOW TO KNOW WHEN YOUR JERKY IS DONE

Jerky is done when you take a piece in your fingers and bend it. It should bend and maybe start to break a little, but it shouldn't snap and break. If the jerky snaps and breaks, it's too dry. You can fix this by dropping the overly dried jerky back into the marinade for an hour or so and then drying it again. This will also give your jerky even more flavor. So, see? It's not such a bad thing after all. Make up a fresh batch of marinade, though. Don't use the old marinade that you had been soaking the raw meat in.

How to Safely Store Jerky

Let's assume that you aren't going to eat every piece of jerky you make immediately after removing it from the heat.

Because so much of the moisture in the meat has been removed, it becomes very shelf stable and could last well up to a month, with proper storage techniques. There are, however, some things to consider when storing your jerky. The more airtight your container, the longer the jerky will last (air and humidity are not friendly toward jerky). The cooler the storage temperature, the longer the jerky will last. To extend the life of your jerky, store it in an airtight container in a cool, dry place. I recommend storing it in the refrigerator. If you want to keep it even longer, drop the container of jerky into your freezer.

Airtight containers include, but are not limited to, resealable plastic bags (with the air removed before sealing them), screw-top jars, and vacuum-sealed packages.

The ingredients in your marinade will also play a role in the shelf life of your jerky. If there are fats in the recipe, or if you don't remove enough of the fat from the meat, it will go bad quicker. Also, if there is a high quantity of sugar in the marinade, the jerky will attract moisture and could go bad more quickly. To help increase the life of these types of jerky, store

them in an airtight container in your refrigerator or freezer. If your jerky is done drying, but still feels oily, or you see glossy spots on it, you need to roll it up into paper towels before packaging it. Simply roll up the jerky in paper toweling, and much of the oil will be absorbed immediately. Unroll and store the jerky pieces in an airtight container. This step will help prolong the life of your jerky.

You can also vacuum-pack your jerky to help increase its shelf life.

There are desiccants (drying agents) that you can use to help rid your jerky of moisture when you have it packed. Just make sure you use *food-grade* desiccants, which are available online..

If you see a bit of mold on a piece of jerky or it starts to taste rancid, the whole batch needs to be thrown out. No trying to save the pieces that you think look okay. Just make another batch.

IS IT SAFE TO MAKE AND EAT HOMEMADE JERKY?

Yes, it's safe to eat homemade jerky. Of course there are some things you need to keep in mind when you're making it.

Temperature is the most important factor when making jerky. It helps kill pathogens, such as *Salmonella* and *E. coli* O157:H7. (Yes, this is even more important than the marinade you choose.) The USDA Meat and Poultry Hotline currently recommends that to safely make jerky, you need to heat the meat to an internal temperature of 160°F and poultry needs to be heated to 165°F before the dehydration process. Once dehydration begins, maintain a constant heat of 130° to 140°F for the remainder of the drying time.[1]

The University of Wisconsin has been researching safe home jerky-making since 1998 (jerky's a pretty big deal in Wisconsin) and has its own recommendations: Dry meat at 145° to 155°F for at least 4 hours, then pop it into an oven that's been preheated to 275°F for 10 minutes. Take it out, let it cool, then pack it up. This postheat treatment will get the meat to an internal temperature of 160°F. The university believes this method to be safe and superior to the USDA method. The USDA method of precooking the meat gives the resulting jerky a crumbly texture . . . not a nice chewy texture, which is preferred by the people of Wisconsin or people anywhere I suspect.

Beyond heat, another way to combat such parasites as *Trichinella* (found in pork and game) is through the freezing of meat. T. spiralis is considered nonviable if the pork is held at 5°F for twenty days before being turned into jerky. Trichinosis is a very small, but still real, potential issue when working with pork, but it's an even bigger issue when you're working with wild game meats. For wild game, the recommendation is cooking to an internal temperature of 170°F. *E. coli* O157:H7 can only be killed through heating to 160°F for beef and 165°F for chicken. Freezing does not effectively kill *E. coli* O157:H7.

Something else that can help cut down on the bad bacteria getting into your jerky is to wear gloves. You can buy a big box of latex or plastic gloves at

1 http://www.fsis.usda.gov/wps/portal/fsis/topics/food-safety-education/get-answers/food-safety-fact-sheets/meat-preparation/jerky-and-food-safety/CT_Index.

cooking or beauty supply stores. They help cut down on any cross-contamination and make cleanup so much easier.

Tips and Tricks to Make Jerky-Making Easier

- Unless directed otherwise mix marinades, dry rubs, and pastes in 1-gallon resealable plastic freezer bags. Add the meat to the bags and remove as much air as possible before sealing and letting everything marinate in the refrigerator. The resealable bags work great for making jerky because they're flexible in size, all of the meat can come in contact with the marinade, and they are relatively inexpensive and disposable (which makes cleanup much easier).

- Remember, everyone has a different tolerance for spicy foods. Read my notes. I'll tell you if it's got any heat in it. If you like it hotter, add more. Removing the seeds and ribs from peppers also helps tone down the heat. Also remember, the fresher your hot pepper powders and seeds, the spicier they will be. As the seasonings age, they lose their heat.

- Use the best and sharpest flat-bladed knife you have. If you don't have one, I highly recommend spending a few extra dollars and getting a good-quality chef's knife. Your hand and arm will thank you and your jerky slices will be beautiful. No serrated blades for cutting jerky because you'll just end up shredding the meat.

- The liquid smoke used in all the recipes that call for liquid smoke is hickory.

- The meats listed in the recipes are those that I felt tasted the best with the marinades. But feel free to use whichever cut of meat you like.

- Regardless of whether you cut your item being dried into slabs or strips, they should be cut between ⅛ and ¼ inch thick.

- The thinner the meat slices, the faster they dry. The more even the size of the meat slices, the more likely everything will be dry at the same time.

- Freezing the meat for 30-45 minutes before slicing helps to make even slicing an easier task.

- Feel free to scrape off any excess marinade, paste, or dry rub before laying the pieces to dry. This will help them to dry more evenly.

- All meats should be trimmed of as much fat as possible.

- Meats should be dried on the 160° to 165°F setting of your electric dehydrator.

- Buy a box of latex or plastic gloves at a restaurant or beauty supply store. They help keep everything clean, offer less chance of cross-contamination, and they help make cleanup easy.

- One pound of fresh meat generally yields around 4 ounces of dried jerky.

CHAPTER 2

Beef

I think I would have to say that beef is the king of jerky. You see far more types of beef jerky in the marketplace than any other kind of jerky.

Remember to choose the leanest cuts of beef when you're making the jerky. Such cuts as sirloin, tenderloin, London broil, top roast, and bottom roast are going to give you the beefiest-tasting and leanest meat you can use. You can use other cuts, but you'll be spending a lot of time cutting out all of the fat and by the time you're done doing that (if your hand hasn't fallen off), you'll most likely be left with a pile of meat shards. So, just stick with the lean cuts, okay?

A few tips to make your jerky-making life easier:

- Use a large cutting board that you can sanitize. Remember to keep your work area, and your hands, clean at all times.

- Frozen or semifrozen meat cuts easier than cold or room-temperature meat. Thirty to 40 minutes before you're ready to make a batch of jerky, drop your meat into the freezer. When it's time, take it out and you'll find that cutting it into ⅛- to ¼-inch even slices is easy peasy.

- It's perfectly fine to make jerky from a piece of meat that you've had in the freezer for a month or two. You'll just need to let it thaw. Don't be concerned by the brown spots you may see on the meat; those happen when meat has been frozen. The meat is fine. Let the meat thaw in the refrigerator in its own time. Do not thaw the meat in the microwave. This can cause the meat to actually cook in spots, and that will change the consistency of your slabs or strips being marinated and dried.

- Sometimes you can find very thinly sliced center cut pork chops at your grocery store. The center cut chops are a part of the loin and they're very lean. They also will save your having to slice the meat, as these are usually sliced to about ¼ inch thick.

- **Electric knives.** Not many people use these anymore, but they can also be used for cutting jerky. I know I said no serrated knives, earlier, but the electric knife is an exception.

- **Deli slicer.** If you're fortunate enough to have one of these machines at your disposal, feel free to use

that. You'll get beautifully even slices and you'll have an easier time cutting meat for slab jerky.

Slab vs. Strip

What's the difference between slab and strip jerky? Slab jerky is generally cut going with the grain of the meat in thin, wide pieces. Slab jerky is very chewy. Strip jerky is cut against the grain and forms a strip that's only as wide as the meat is high. Strip jerky is tender and easy to chew. Feel free to cut your jerky any way you like.

Ground Meats

Ground meat jerky is a pretty popular jerky choice for people because it's so much easier to chew (no real jaw workout). At the store, ground meat jerky comes in strips and round lengths that are almost like meat ropes. For the purposes of this book, we'll be sticking to making the strips, since the ropes and shapes take longer to dry. But shapes can be made with the ground meat.

Any meat that you would use for making strip or slab jerky can be used in making ground meat jerky. When buying ground beef for jerky making, I always by a minimum 90/10 meat, which means it's made up of 90 percent lean meat and 10 percent fat. If I can find a mixture of 93/7, I'll buy that instead.

A few tips to make your ground meat jerky-making life easier:

- Always start by putting your ground meat in the mixing bowl first, then add your seasonings. This makes it a lot easier to get everything evenly blended. You don't want to bite into a piece that only tastes like garlic and nothing else, do you?

- Use your hands to blend the mixture. I know it sounds gross and icky, but it really is the best way to get everything evenly blended without overworking the meat. Hey, you can always put on some gloves (that's what I do).

- Let the meat rest for 10 to 15 minutes after you get everything mixed. This lets the seasonings begin to work their way into the meat.

- To roll out the jerky, lay a large piece of parchment paper on your counter, then add your meat mixture on top. Pull off a large piece of plastic wrap and lay it over the top of the meat. Gently start to press the meat out with your hands. Straighten the top layer of plastic wrap, then grab your rolling pin and roll out the meat.

- Do not thaw ground meat in the microwave. This can cause the meat to actually cook in spots and that will change the consistency and flavor of your jerky.

- Roll out the meat ⅛ to ¼ inch thick.

- If drying in the oven, just place the parchment paper (with the meat on it) on a baking sheet, remove the plastic wrap, score the meat, and pop the sheet into the oven.

- If drying in a dehydrator, cut the meat into slices and use an offset spatula to put the slices onto the fruit rollup drying sheet.

- If you use an extruder, follow the instructions that came with it.

Cowboy Steak Jerky

I live in Dallas now, so I thought it was only appropriate to make a cowboy steak version of jerky. I've even used the traditional ingredients found in most cowboy steak recipes, so as soon as you bite into it you'll get that familiar flavor. Sorry, I can't guarantee you'll get your cowboy steak jerky served to you on traditional cowboy enamelware or even eat it with a real Wrangler-wearing cowboy. But I promise that it will still taste delicious.

INGREDIENTS

1 tablespoon instant espresso powder

1 tablespoon kosher salt

2 teaspoons brown sugar

1 teaspoon chipotle powder

1 teaspoon paprika

½ teaspoon dry mustard

½ teaspoon ground black pepper

1 pound London broil strips

INSTRUCTIONS

1. In a small bowl, thoroughly mix together all the ingredients, except the meat. Place the meat strips in a 1-gallon resealable plastic freezer bag and add the dry rub. Mix the strips around so the meat gets completely coated with the dry rub. Remove as much air as possible from the bag, seal, and place it in the refrigerator for 8 to 24 hours. During the marinating time, remove the bag from the refrigerator and work the meat around so the rub is fully incorporated into it. Remove the strips from the rub and arrange in a single layer in your choice of dryer. Dry as directed on pages 16–19.

Kicked-Up BBQ Jerky

This is what you get when you take your favorite BBQ sauce and add ingredients to it to kick it into overdrive. I wanted the sauce to have a richer flavor, so I added some Worcestershire sauce and whiskey to it. I also thought it needed a bit of heat to tame its sweetness. Helllloooo . . . Tabasco. The finished jerky has a great BBQ flavor that's not too spicy. It's a wet jerky, so the sticky bits that are left on your fingers make the flavor last a little bit longer.

INGREDIENTS

½ cup Sweet Baby Ray's BBQ Sauce (regular flavor)

2 tablespoons soy sauce

2 tablespoons whiskey

1 teaspoon Tabasco sauce

1 teaspoon Worcestershire sauce

1 pound London broil strips

INSTRUCTIONS

1. In a 1-gallon resealable plastic freezer bag, thoroughly mix together all the ingredients, except the meat, and allow the mixture to rest for 10 minutes. Add the meat strips to the marinade and mix them around so they get completely coated with the marinade. Remove as much air as possible from the bag, seal, and place it in the refrigerator for 8 to 24 hours. During the marinating time, remove the bag from the refrigerator and work the meat around so the marinade is fully incorporated into it. Remove the strips from the marinade and arrange in a single layer in your choice of dryer. Dry as directed on pages 16–19.

Kung Pao Beef Jerky

While you might think this would be a hot and spicy jerky, it isn't. The Sichuan peppers have a very fruity/citrusy flavor that tastes delicious with the salt, ginger, and sherry in this recipe. Using whole red chiles, instead of red pepper flakes, keeps this from going from flavorful to blow-your-face-off hot. Of course, if you're a chile head, you can add more red peppers and make it as hot as you want.

INGREDIENTS

½ cup soy sauce

½ cup sherry

10 dried red chiles, broken up

2 tablespoons Szechuan peppercorns, crushed

1 tablespoon granulated garlic

1 tablespoon ground ginger

1½ tablespoons sugar

1 to 1½ pounds London broil strips

INSTRUCTIONS

1. In a 1-gallon resealable plastic freezer bag, thoroughly mix together all the ingredients, except the meat, and allow the mixture to rest for 10 minutes. Add the meat strips to the marinade and mix them around so they get completely coated with the marinade. Remove as much air as possible from the bag, seal, and place it in the refrigerator for 8 to 24 hours. During the marinating time, remove the bag from the refrigerator a few times and work the meat around so the marinade is fully incorporated into it. Remove the strips from the marinade and arrange in a single layer in your choice of dryer. Dry as directed on pages 16–19.

Fast Tex-Mex Jerky

Sometimes you just don't want to wait to stuff your face with jerky.
If you've got a microwave, deli meat, and taco seasoning in your kitchen, you're more than halfway to jerky nirvana. Made in just minutes, this jerky has lots of great South of the Border flavors and lets you begin eating it in under an hour. Of course, that presumes you have the ingredients on hand. If not, you'll have to probably add another 30 minutes before you enter jerky heaven.

INGREDIENTS

½ cup vegetable juice, such as V8
1½ tablespoons taco seasoning mix
Cholula hot sauce
1 pound deli sliced roast beef, cut into strips

INSTRUCTIONS

1. In a 1-gallon resealable plastic freezer bag, thoroughly mix together all the ingredients, except the meat, adding the hot sauce to taste, and allow the mixture to rest for 10 minutes. Add the meat strips to the marinade and mix them around so they get completely coated with the marinade. Remove as much air as possible from the bag, seal, and place it in the refrigerator for 30 minutes. Line a microwave bacon cooker or microwave-safe dish with a layer of paper towels. Remove the meat from the marinade and arrange it in a single layer on the paper towels. Cover the meat with another paper towel and put into the microwave. Cook for 2½ minutes on high, then flip the meat over, re-cover, and cook for another 1½ minutes on high. Repeat this step one more time. If the jerky is done to your liking, let it cool, then eat. Otherwise repeat the cooking steps in 30-second intervals until the desired doneness is reached.

Spicy Chocolate Jerky

Chocolate and jerky seem to be a highly unlikely pairing, you would think. But have you ever heard of Mexican mole? Mole is a Mexican sauce that's served with meat and has anywhere from sixteen to thirty ingredients in it . . . including quite a lot of chocolate. This spicy chocolate jerky doesn't have nearly that many ingredients in it, but I think it's just as delicious. Plus, it's a lot less likely to drip down your shirt. No, this is not going to taste like a candy bar.

INGREDIENTS

2 tablespoons unsweetened cocoa powder

1½ tablespoons kosher salt

1 tablespoon sugar

1½ teaspoons chili powder

1 teaspoon ground cinnamon

1 teaspoon ground nutmeg

¼ teaspoon cayenne pepper

1 to 1½ pounds London broil strips

INSTRUCTIONS

1. In a small bowl, thoroughly mix together all the ingredients, except the meat, and allow the mixture to rest for 10 minutes. Place the meat strips in a 1-gallon resealable plastic freezer bag with the dry rub. Mix the strips around so the meat gets completely coated with the dry rub. Remove as much air as possible from the bag, seal, and place it in the refrigerator for 8 to 24 hours. During the marinating time, remove the bag from the refrigerator and work the meat around so the rub is fully incorporated into it. Remove the strips from the rub and arrange in a single layer in your choice of dryer. Dry as directed on pages 16–19.

Margaritatown Jerky

An icy cold margarita, a basket of chips and salsa, a few tacos, and a bright, sunny day sounds about perfect, doesn't it? Well, I thought I would skip all of those individual items (too many dishes to wash) and roll it all together in a batch of jerky. You get the taste of tequila, the lip-smacking goodness of a splash of lime, the salt, and meat to satisfy your hunger—all in one bite. Serve your chips and salsa separately.

INGREDIENTS

⅓ cup + 2 tablespoons lime juice

⅓ cup tequila

¼ cup orange juice

2 tablespoons salt

2 tablespoons sugar

1 to 1½ pounds London broil strips

INSTRUCTIONS

1. In a 1-gallon resealable plastic freezer bag, thoroughly mix together all the ingredients, except the meat, and allow the mixture to rest for 10 minutes. Add the meat strips to the marinade and mix them around so they get completely coated with the marinade. Remove as much air as possible from the bag, seal, and place it in the refrigerator for 4 to 6 hours. During the marinating time, remove the bag from the refrigerator and work the meat around so the marinade is fully incorporated into it. Do not leave the meat to marinate longer than 6 hours or the lime juice may cause it to turn mushy. Remove the strips from the marinade and arrange in a single layer in your choice of dryer. Dry as directed on pages 16–19.

Maple Leaf Jerky

We give our neighbors to the north a lot of grief sometimes, but how could we not love them for two of their finest exports (and I'm not including Justin Bieber as one of them). I'm talking about maple syrup and Canadian whisky (no e), of course. I put these two delicious Canadian exports together to make a jerky that's got a touch of maple sweetness and a hint of smoke from the whisky. It'll have you singing "O Canada" after just a piece or two. No guarantee you'll be singing it in tune, though.

INGREDIENTS

⅔ cup Canadian whisky

⅓ cup + 2 tablespoons pure maple syrup (grade B)

3 tablespoons kosher salt

¼ teaspoon ground black pepper

4 star anise, broken up

1½ to 2 pounds London broil strips

INSTRUCTIONS

1. In a 1-gallon resealable plastic freezer bag, thoroughly mix together all the ingredients, except the meat, and allow the mixture to rest for 10 minutes. Add the meat strips to the marinade and mix them around so they get completely coated with the marinade. Remove as much air as possible from the bag, seal, and place it in the refrigerator for 8 to 24 hours. During the marinating time, remove the bag from the refrigerator and work the meat around so the marinade is fully incorporated into it. Remove the strips from the marinade and arrange in a single layer in your choice of dryer. Dry as directed on pages 16–19.

Black and Tan, a.k.a. The Half and Half Jerky

History lesson: In America, there's a beer cocktail consisting of a dark stout or porter beer "floating" on top of a lighter-colored lager beer; we call this a Black and Tan, and drink a lot of them on St. Patrick's Day. In Ireland, this term is a no-no and it's called a Half and Half. I couldn't resist mixing these rich flavors with a good cut of beef and drying it to perfection. I must admit, it does make a really great bar snack for when you're drinking the liquid version of this.

INGREDIENTS

1½ cups Guinness stout

2 tablespoons brown sugar

1 tablespoon unsweetened cocoa powder

1 tablespoon kosher salt

1 teaspoon vanilla extract

1 pound eye of round strips

INSTRUCTIONS

1. In a 1-gallon resealable plastic freezer bag, thoroughly mix together all the ingredients, except the meat, and allow the mixture to rest for 10 minutes. Add the meat strips to the marinade and mix them around so they get completely coated with the marinade. Remove as much air as possible from the bag, seal, and place it in the refrigerator for 8 to 24 hours. During the marinating time, remove the bag from the refrigerator and work the meat around so the marinade is fully incorporated into it. Remove the strips from the marinade and arrange in a single layer in your choice of dryer. Dry as directed on pages 16–19.

Honey Whiskey Peppercorn Jerky

I mix up all kinds of whiskey libations, from the classics to my own variations. I'm a sucker for brown liquors. For this jerky, I took a bunch of crushed peppercorns and brought out more of the heat in the whiskey, while still allowing some of the sweet honey flavor to come through. This one will put some hair on your chest.

INGREDIENTS

- ½ cup Jack Daniels Tennessee Honey
- 2 tablespoons kosher salt
- 2 tablespoons brown sugar
- 1½ tablespoons crushed black peppercorns
- 1 pound cross rib steak strips

INSTRUCTIONS

1. In a 1-gallon resealable plastic freezer bag, thoroughly mix together all the ingredients, except the meat, and allow the mixture to rest for 10 minutes. Add the meat strips to the marinade and mix them around so they get completely coated with the marinade. Remove as much air as possible from the bag, seal, and place it in the refrigerator for 8 to 24 hours. During the marinating time, remove the bag from the refrigerator and work the meat around so the marinade is fully incorporated into it. Remove the strips from the marinade and arrange in a single layer in your choice of dryer. Dry as directed on pages 16–19.

Beef Kalbi Jerky

Korean grilled short ribs have gotten really popular in the past few years. They're so popular you even find them on restaurant menus that don't have another single Korean dish on them. While this beef *kalbi* jerky tastes like the traditional dish (it's got soy sauce, ginger, sesame, and sugar), it's made with a much leaner cut of beef. Since it's jerky, there are no bones, either.

INGREDIENTS

¾ cup soy sauce

½ cup sugar

2 tablespoons sesame oil

2 teaspoons grated fresh ginger

3 garlic cloves, grated

½ medium-size onion, chopped

1 to 1½ pounds London broil strips

INSTRUCTIONS

1. In a 1-gallon resealable plastic freezer bag, thoroughly mix together all the ingredients, except the meat, and allow the mixture to rest for 10 minutes. Add the meat strips to the marinade and mix them around so they get completely coated with the marinade. Remove as much air as possible from the bag, seal, and place it in the refrigerator for 8 to 24 hours. During the marinating time, remove the bag from the refrigerator and work the meat around so the marinade is fully incorporated into it. Remove the strips from the marinade and arrange in a single layer in your choice of dryer. Dry as directed on pages 16–19.

Carne Asada Jerky

Carne asada is a popular dish of marinated and quick cooked flank steak from South of the Border, served in tacos or burritos. But to make this jerky you don't need to have your passport and you don't even need to find a tortilla. With a few ingredients for the marinade, some thinly cut London broil, and a little time in the dehydrator, your carne asada jerky will be ready to eat in no time. Just think of all the carbs you'll save by leaving out the tortillas.

INGREDIENTS

1 tablespoon lime juice

2 teaspoons kosher salt

1 teaspoon brown sugar

¾ teaspoon dried oregano

¾ teaspoon granulated garlic

½ teaspoon ground coriander

¼ teaspoon ground cumin

¼ teaspoon onion powder

¼ teaspoon ground black pepper

½ to 1 serrano chile pepper, mashed

1 pound London broil strips

INSTRUCTIONS

1. In a 1-gallon resealable plastic freezer bag, thoroughly mix together all the ingredients, except the meat, and allow the mixture to rest for 10 minutes. Add the meat strips to the marinade and mix them around so they get completely coated with the marinade. Remove as much air as possible from the bag, seal, and place it in the refrigerator for 8 to 24 hours. During the marinating time, remove the bag from the refrigerator and work the meat around so the marinade is fully incorporated into it. Remove the strips from the marinade and arrange in a single layer in your choice of dryer. Drying time for this recipe is 3 to 5 hours.

43

Cherry Chipotle Jerky

Chocolate, cherries, and chipotle chiles are a triumvirate of amazingness. The sweetness of the cherries combined with the smoky chipotle is a real winner. Plus you get the added benefit of the spicy kick from the chipotle. Then that bit of cocoa flavor (it's not sweet) adds a richness to the whole thing. Putting them together to coat strips of beef is pure genius, if I do say so myself. Genius!

INGREDIENTS

2 cups unsweetened cherry juice

⅓ cup ketchup

⅓ cup brown sugar

¼ cup lime juice

1 tablespoon kosher salt

2 teaspoons unsweetened cocoa powder

1 teaspoon chipotle powder

A few grinds of black pepper

1 to 1 ½ pounds London broil strips

INSTRUCTIONS

1. Pour the cherry juice into a small pan and heat over medium-high heat until it has reduced to 1 cup, 10 to 15 minutes. Let the juice cool to room temperature, then proceed. In a 1-gallon resealable plastic freezer bag, thoroughly mix together all the ingredients, except the meat, and allow the mixture to rest for 10 minutes. Add the meat strips to the marinade and mix them around so they get completely coated with the marinade. Remove as much air as possible from the bag, seal, and place it in the refrigerator for 8 to 24 hours. During the marinating time, remove the bag from the refrigerator and work the meat around so the marinade is fully incorporated into it. Remove the strips from the marinade and arrange in a single layer in your choice of dryer. Dry as directed on pages 16–19.

Roasted Garlic Pepper Jerky

Do you know what happens when you roast garlic? Sure, it gets soft and mushy, but it also gets really sweet and loses that bite fresh garlic has. This jerky takes lots of that sweet roasted garlic and combines it with brown sugar and soy sauce to give this jerky a richness you'd expect to get from a well-grilled steak—not a simple little piece of jerky. Prepare to be wowed.

INGREDIENTS

2 heads of garlic (about 20 cloves, total)

2 tablespoons olive oil

Pinch of salt

Pinch of ground black pepper

1 cup soy sauce

½ cup Worcestershire sauce

¼ cup brown sugar

¾ teaspoon ground black pepper

1 ½ pounds London broil strips

INSTRUCTIONS

1. To roast the garlic, preheat the oven to 350°F. Cut about ¼ inch off the top of the garlic heads (so you can see the cloves inside). Place the heads in a double layer of foil. Drizzle the olive oil over the tops of the garlic and sprinkle with the salt and black pepper. Fold the foil around garlic heads so they are sealed in. Roast for 55 minutes. Remove from the oven and let cool until you can handle the cloves. Once cooled, squeeze the cloves into a food processor and proceed.

2. Toss all the remaining ingredients, except the meat, into the food processor and buzz until everything is pureed. Pour the puree into a 1-gallon resealable plastic freezer bag and allow the mixture to rest for 10 minutes. Add the meat strips to the marinade and mix them around so they get completely coated with the marinade. Remove as much air as possible from the bag, seal, and place it in the refrigerator for 8 to 24 hours. During the marinating time, remove the bag from the refrigerator and work the meat around so the marinade is fully incorporated with the strips. Remove the strips from the marinade and arrange in a single layer in your choice of dryer. Dry as directed on pages 16–19.

Habanero Mango Jerky

I can't make enough of this jerky to satisfy everyone's cravings.

Several years ago, we met a man named Randy who owned a fantastic chili restaurant in the Valley. Every day, he served up thirteen different types of chili that took him three to four days to make. Our favorite was habanero mango. On his heat scale, this chili was a 10 out of 10 but the sweetness of the mango and the actual flavor of the habanero were just too tempting to pass up. Randy has since passed away and the chili place has closed, but this jerky is my homage to his fantastically amazing chili. Here's to you Randy.

INGREDIENTS

1 large mango, pitted, peeled, and cut into chunks

1 medium-size onion, roughly chopped

3 habanero peppers

2 tablespoons lemon juice

1½ tablespoons white vinegar

1 tablespoon sugar

2 garlic cloves, minced

2 teaspoons kosher salt

1 to 1½ pounds London broil strips

INSTRUCTIONS

1. Toss all the ingredients, except the meat, into a food processor and buzz until everything is pureed. Pour the puree into a 1-gallon resealable plastic freezer bag and allow the mixture to rest for 10 minutes. Add the meat strips to the marinade and mix them around so they get completely coated with the marinade. Remove as much air as possible from the bag, seal, and place it in the refrigerator for 8 to 24 hours. During the marinating time, remove the bag from the refrigerator and work the meat around so the marinade is fully incorporated with the strips. Remove the strips from the marinade and arrange in a single layer in your choice of dryer. You can reduce the number of habanero peppers to cut down on the heat. Dry as directed on pages 16–19.

Sweet Heat Sriracha Jerky

What can I say about this one?

Sriracha sauce has gotten to be almost as popular as bacon, so I had to make a sriracha jerky. You'll be pleasantly surprised that the heat from the sauce kind of disappears in this recipe, so even if you don't do spicy, you can eat this jerky. Yes, sriracha sauce is more than just a red blob of hot sauce. Now you can really taste it. If you want to add some heat to this, toss in some red pepper flakes. The flavor will blend better than if you added another type of hot sauce.

INGREDIENTS

½ cup unseasoned rice vinegar

⅓ cup + 2 tablespoons sriracha sauce

¼ cup brown sugar

2 teaspoons granulated ginger

1 teaspoon granulated garlic

1 teaspoon salt

1 pound London broil strips

INSTRUCTIONS

1. In a 1-gallon resealable plastic freezer bag, thoroughly mix together all the ingredients, except the meat, and allow the mixture to rest for 10 minutes. Add the meat strips to the marinade and mix them around so they get completely coated with the marinade. Remove as much air as possible from the bag, seal, and place it in the refrigerator for 8 to 24 hours. During the marinating time, remove the bag from the refrigerator and work the meat around so the marinade is fully incorporated into it. Remove the strips from the marinade and arrange in a single layer in your choice of dryer. Dry as directed on pages 16–19.

Whiskey Pete Jerky

A certain law enforcement group went bananas when I gave its members some of this jerky. I even had to make them more (I didn't want to risk ending up on a "most wanted" poster). This is a truly simple jerky, but the flavors of all the ingredients really come through. You'll also have a better understanding of why whiskey drinks sell so well at steak houses. Whiskey and beef are a match made in heaven.

INGREDIENTS

½ cup brown sugar

½ cup whiskey

½ cup soy sauce

¼ cup cider vinegar

1 tablespoon Worcestershire sauce

4 drops liquid hickory smoke

1 pound London broil strips

INSTRUCTIONS

1. In a 1-gallon resealable plastic freezer bag, thoroughly mix together all the ingredients, except the meat, and allow the mixture to rest for 10 minutes. Add the meat strips to the marinade and mix them around so they get completely coated with the marinade. Remove as much air as possible from the bag, seal, and place it in the refrigerator for 8 to 24 hours. During the marinating time, remove the bag from the refrigerator and work the meat around so the marinade is fully incorporated into it. Remove the strips from the marinade and arrange in a single layer in your choice of dryer. Dry as directed on pages 16–19.

Taco Tuesday Jerky

Don't be put off by the number of ingredients in this recipe. I know it looks daunting. You're basically making your own taco seasoning (hint, hint . . . you could use this on actual taco meat when you make tacos at home). This one took some time to perfect. The tomato powder is easily found (and inexpensive) in stores or on the Internet, and you'll find quite a few uses for it once you start using it. A handful of this jerky will have you reaching for a margarita, so make sure the tequila is close by.

INGREDIENTS

2 tablespoons chili powder

4 teaspoons brown sugar

4 teaspoons tomato powder

1 tablespoon smoked paprika

1 teaspoon kosher salt

2 teaspoons dried oregano

1½ teaspoons ground cumin

1½ teaspoons ground coriander

1½ teaspoons onion powder

1½ teaspoons garlic powder

½ teaspoon citric acid (gives it that squeeze of lime flavor)

⅛ teaspoon ground black pepper

1 pound London broil strips

INSTRUCTIONS

1. In a small bowl, thoroughly mix together all the ingredients, except the meat. Place the meat strips in a 1-gallon resealable plastic freezer bag and add the dry rub. Mix the strips around so the meat gets completely coated with the dry rub. Remove as much air as possible from the bag, seal, and place it in the refrigerator for 8 to 24 hours. During the marinating time, remove the bag from the refrigerator and work the meat around so the rub is fully incorporated into it. Remove the strips from the rub and arrange in a single layer in your choice of dryer. Dry as directed on pages 16–19.

Teriyaki Jerky

This is one of the most traditional jerky flavors you can eat. Sure, I could have just said to pour a bottle of your favorite teriyaki sauce over the meat and sent you on your way, but making your own teriyaki tastes soooo much better. I use fresh ginger in this recipe because it makes a huge difference in the overall flavor of the sauce, so no powdered ginger, please. Wait until you taste how good a homemade teriyaki sauce tastes. It really does make a difference.

INGREDIENTS

¼ cup soy sauce

¼ cup mirin

2 tablespoons water

2 tablespoons sugar

1 tablespoon brown sugar

1 tablespoon grated fresh ginger

2 garlic cloves, crushed

1 pound London broil strips

INSTRUCTIONS

1. In a 1-gallon resealable plastic freezer bag, thoroughly mix together all the ingredients, except the meat, and allow the mixture to rest for 10 minutes. Add the meat strips to the marinade and mix them around so they get completely coated with the marinade. Remove as much air as possible from the bag, seal, and place it in the refrigerator for 8 to 24 hours. During the marinating time, remove the bag from the refrigerator and work the meat around so the marinade is fully incorporated into it. Remove the strips from the marinade and arrange in a single layer in your choice of dryer. Dry as directed on pages 16–19.

Carne Asada Jerky II

I call this one Carne Asada Part Dos. There's definitely more than one carne asada recipe out there, so I thought I'd give you another one. This recipe is full of citrusy flavors, such as orange and lime, with a touch of Mexican beer tossed in for good measure. This carne asada jerky is much lighter tasting than the other recipe because it has more fresh ingredients and less dried spices. Olé!

INGREDIENTS

1 cup Mexican beer

½ cup orange juice

2 tablespoons lime juice

2 garlic cloves, crushed

½ medium-size red onion, chopped

1 tablespoon brown sugar

1 tablespoon kosher salt

A few grinds of black pepper

Small handful of fresh cilantro (including stems), roughly chopped

1 pound London broil strips

INSTRUCTIONS

1. Toss all the ingredients, except the meat, into a food processor and buzz until everything is pureed. Pour the puree into a 1-gallon resealable plastic freezer bag and allow the mixture to rest for 10 minutes. Add the meat strips to the marinade and mix them around so they get completely coated with the marinade. Remove as much air as possible from the bag, seal, and place it in the refrigerator for 4 to 6 hours. During the marinating time, remove the bag from the refrigerator and work the meat around so the marinade is fully incorporated into it. Remove the strips from the marinade and arrange in a single layer in your choice of dryer. Dry as directed on pages 16–19.

Whiskey Neat Jerky

This is the redneck cousin of **Whiskey Pete.** Sometimes you just want simple, and it doesn't get much simpler than this. Whiskey, meat, and salt. To say that you can taste the whiskey in this recipe would be a massive understatement. But simple is as simple does . . . . Cheers!

INGREDIENTS

1 cup whiskey

1 pound London broil strips

Kosher salt

INSTRUCTIONS

1. Pour the whiskey into a 1-gallon resealable plastic freezer bag and add the meat strips. Mix them around so they get completely coated with the whiskey. Remove as much air as possible from the bag, seal, and place it in the refrigerator for 8 to 24 hours. During the marinating time, remove the bag from the refrigerator and work the meat around so the whiskey is fully incorporated into it. Remove the strips from the whiskey and arrange in a single layer in your choice of dryer. Sprinkle kosher salt onto the meat strips before drying. Dry as directed on pages 16–19.

Philly Cheese Steak Jerky

Short of traveling to Philadelphia, this is the closest you're going to get to authentic Philly cheese steak flavor (in jerky form). I'm not even sure you can get cheese steak jerky in Philly. The cheddar cheese powder can be purchased online or at your local grocery store (in the popcorn aisle). Minus the roll and a long line of people in front of you ordering, you'll swear you're eating a real Philly cheese steak. For the full effect, eat this jerky outside when the temps fall below freezing.

INGREDIENTS

¼ cup Cheddar cheese powder

½ cup soy sauce

1 tablespoon Worcestershire sauce

¼ teaspoon granulated garlic

⅛ teaspoon cayenne pepper

A few grinds of black pepper

1 pound London broil strips

INSTRUCTIONS

1. In a 1-gallon resealable plastic freezer bag, thoroughly mix together all the ingredients, except the meat, and allow the mixture to rest for 10 minutes. Add the meat strips to the marinade and mix them around so they get completely coated with the marinade. Remove as much air as possible from the bag, seal, and place it in the refrigerator for 8 to 24 hours. During the marinating time, remove the bag from the refrigerator and work the meat around so the marinade is fully incorporated into it. Remove the strips from the marinade and arrange in a single layer in your choice of dryer. Dry as directed on pages 16–19.

Southwest WOW Jerky

A mere mention of the Southwest conjures up visions of desert, cactus, and chiles, or maybe coyotes and crazy roadrunners. I've used a couple of different chiles in this one, Hatch chile and cayenne. The Hatch chile gives you that great Southwest flavor of chile (without the roaring heat) and the hit of cayenne gives you the bit of spice you're looking for in Southwest food. The rest of the ingredients that round out this jerky give it a rich and robust flavor that will keep your lips smacking for quite a while. No, it's not rude to smack your lips when eating jerky . . . it's expected.

INGREDIENTS

½ cup soy sauce

1 (4-ounce) can diced, or 3 roasted Hatch chiles, chopped or sliced

2 teaspoons sugar

½ teaspoon onion powder

⅜ teaspoon granulated garlic

¼ teaspoon ground cumin

¼ teaspoon cayenne pepper

1 pound London broil strips

INSTRUCTIONS

1. Toss all the ingredients, except the meat, into a food processor and buzz until everything is pureed. Pour the puree into a 1-gallon resealable plastic freezer bag and allow the mixture to rest for 10 minutes. Add the meat strips to the marinade and mix them around so they get completely coated with the marinade. Remove as much air as possible from the bag, seal, and place it in the refrigerator for 8 to 24 hours. During the marinating time, remove the bag from the refrigerator and work the meat around so the marinade is fully incorporated into it. Remove the strips from the marinade and arrange in a single layer in your choice of dryer. Dry as directed on pages 16–19.

Biltong

Biltong is what the British and South Africans call their jerky.

However, true South African _biltong_ isn't exactly like American jerky. While they use different seasonings (coriander, baking soda, and vinegar as the preservative instead of salt), they also don't dry it as completely as what U.S. jerky eaters are used to. So it has a softer consistency and needs to be eaten more quickly. That being said, numerous _biltong_ stores in South Africa use the traditional seasoning but cut the meat into slices and dry it all the way through the way U.S. jerky eaters are used to. Of course, they use some different animals over there, too. I've also included a recipe for the completely dried _biltong_, since South Africans typically eat the thoroughly dried jerky when going on game drives through Kruger Park.

INGREDIENTS

2 tablespoons kosher salt

2 tablespoons brown sugar

1½ tablespoons coriander seeds, crushed

1 teaspoon baking soda

1 to 1½ pounds London broil

3 tablespoons red wine vinegar

¼ teaspoon ground black pepper

1 quart water

½ cup white vinegar

INSTRUCTIONS

1. Mix the salt, brown sugar, coriander, and baking soda together in a small bowl. Slice the meat into 2-inch-wide strips, cut with the grain. Liberally coat the meat with the dry mixture. Arrange the meat in a single layer on a plate large enough to hold the strips and drizzle the meat with the red wine vinegar. You'll see a bit of fizzing (that's from the baking soda). Cover tightly with plastic wrap and refrigerate overnight. Mix the water and white vinegar in a large bowl.

2. Dip the meat strips into the vinegar solution (which will pull off a lot of the big pieces of the rub) and place on a single layer in your dryer. Dry as directed on pages 16–19. Because of the thickness of the meat, drying for 6 to 8 hours will not dry it completely through and that's the style of this jerky. This doesn't keep as long as other jerkies and must be refrigerated. Cut into individual pieces, against the grain, for eating. Eat within 7 days. This jerky will still be red in the middle when you cut into it. Not bleeding, but it will be undercooked.

Biltong II

This is the dried version resembling the jerky you're more familiar with.

INGREDIENTS

2 tablespoons kosher salt

2 tablespoons brown sugar

1½ tablespoons coriander seeds, crushed

1 teaspoon baking soda

¼ teaspoon ground black pepper

1 pound London broil strips

3 tablespoons red wine vinegar

1 quart water

½ cup white vinegar

INSTRUCTIONS

1. Mix the salt, brown sugar, coriander, baking soda, and black pepper together in a small bowl. Slice the meat into ¼-inch strips, against the grain. Liberally coat the meat with the dry mixture. Arrange the meat in a single layer on a plate large enough to hold the strips and drizzle the meat with the red wine vinegar. You can stack the strips on top of each other in a crisscross pattern, but make sure to drizzle with vinegar before laying any meat on top of another piece of meat. You'll see a bit of fizzing (that's from the baking soda). Cover tightly with plastic wrap and refrigerate overnight.

2. Mix the water and white vinegar in a large bowl. Dip the meat strips into the vinegar solution (which will pull off a lot of the big pieces of the rub) and place on a single layer in your dryer. Dry as directed on pages 16–19.

Horseradish Jerky

Do you like prime rib? Do you like going to one of those restaurants where they slice pieces off a huge hunk of meat? Then, you're really going to like this horseradish jerky because it tastes just like a jerkied version of your favorite prime rib dinner. Herbs, like those they use when they roast the beast, combined with horseradish that you use at the table, make this a jerky delicacy. Sorry, there's no *jus* available for this one and no sneeze guard is involved with getting pieces of this, either.

INGREDIENTS

¼ cup grated fresh horseradish (*not* horseradish sauce)

2 tablespoons white wine vinegar

2 tablespoons kosher salt

½ teaspoon dried rosemary

2 teaspoons dried thyme

1¼ teaspoons grated garlic cloves

½ teaspoon ground black pepper

1 to 1½ pounds London broil strips

INSTRUCTIONS

1. In a 1-gallon resealable plastic freezer bag, thoroughly mix together all the ingredients, except the meat, and allow the mixture to rest for 10 minutes. Add the meat strips to the paste and mix them around so they get completely coated with the marinade. Remove as much air as possible from the bag, seal, and place it in the refrigerator for 8 to 24 hours. During the marinating time, remove the bag from the refrigerator and work the meat around so the paste is fully incorporated into it. Remove the strips from the paste and arrange in a single layer in your choice of dryer. Dry as directed on pages 16–19.

Kimchi Jerky

Kimchi, that odiferous fermented cabbage Korean condiment that's become all the rage lately, has now found its way into jerky. You're welcome! The flavor of kimchi is like nothing else. That combination of heat and vegetables gives you sweetness, lots of flavor, and of course heat. Because it's normally served alongside meat, I thought we should just infuse the meat with the kimchi flavor. Unfortunately, the heat gets lost during the infusion. Which is good for those of you who find kimchi to be too spicy. But if you like the heat, just add some red pepper flakes to the marinade and you'll be all set. Heat and flavor—ta-dah!

INGREDIENTS

1 (28-ounce) jar kimchi

1 pound London broil strips

Red pepper flakes (optional)

INSTRUCTIONS

1. Place the kimchi in a 1-gallon resealable plastic freezer bag. Add the meat strips to the kimchi and mix them around so they all get coated with the kimchi. Add the red pepper flakes, if using. Remove as much air as possible from the bag, seal, and place it in the refrigerator for 8 to 24 hours. During the marinating time, remove the bag from the refrigerator and work the meat around so the kimchi is fully incorporated into it. Remove from the kimchi and arrange in a single layer in your choice of dryer. Dry as directed on pages 16–19.

Orange Beef Jerky

Is this one of your favorite take-out dishes at your local Chinese restaurants? If so, you'll love the jerky version. There's lots of orange but also lots of heat from Thai bird chiles. I tried several other types of chiles, but they just didn't cut it. An added benefit of this jerky? Since it's not fried, like the traditional recipe, it's much healthier for you. And we're all about healthy here . . . right?

INGREDIENTS

½ cup orange juice

2 dried Thai bird chiles, crushed

2 tablespoons soy sauce

1 tablespoon brown sugar

1 tablespoon grated fresh ginger

1 tablespoon Szechuan peppercorns, crushed

1 tablespoon unseasoned rice vinegar

2 teaspoons orange zest

1 teaspoon sesame oil

1 pound London broil strips

INSTRUCTIONS

1. In a 1-gallon resealable plastic freezer bag, thoroughly mix together all the ingredients, except the meat, and allow the mixture to rest for 10 minutes. Add the meat strips to the marinade and mix them around so they get completely coated with the marinade. Remove as much air as possible from the bag, seal, and place it in the refrigerator for 8 to 24 hours. During the marinating time, remove the bag from the refrigerator and work the meat around so the marinade is fully incorporated into it. Remove the strips from the marinade and arrange in a single layer in your choice of dryer. Dry as directed on pages 16–19.

Bacon-Wrapped Filet Mignon Jerky

I know that I preach about using really lean cuts of meat, and most people don't think of filet mignon as being lean, but it is quite lean. That's why it's so easily messed up at restaurants. Lots of people like their filet wrapped in bacon (the fat helps keep the meat moist). But we've already talked about how bacon doesn't really work for homemade jerky, so this jerky has a bacon flavor mixed into the seasonings. Viva le filet! Cut the filet into slabs to savor the flavor even longer.

INGREDIENTS

3 tablespoons liquid aminos

2 tablespoons pure maple syrup (grade B)

2 tablespoons cider vinegar

1 teaspoon paprika

½ teaspoon smoked paprika

½ teaspoon ground black pepper

4 drops liquid hickory smoke

1 pound filet mignon, cut into slabs

INSTRUCTIONS

1. In a 1-gallon resealable plastic freezer bag, thoroughly mix together all the ingredients, except the meat, and allow the mixture to rest for 10 minutes. Add the meat strips to the marinade and mix them around so they get completely coated with the marinade. Remove as much air as possible from the bag, seal, and place it in the refrigerator for 8 to 24 hours. During the marinating time, remove the bag from the refrigerator and work the meat around so the marinade is fully incorporated into it. Remove the strips from the marinade and arrange in a single layer in your choice of dryer. Dry as directed on pages 16–19.

Honey Chipotle Jerky

I can't resist the heat and smoke that comes from a smoked and dried jalapeño. So here's another recipe using chipotle peppers. The rich sweetness of honey combined with the smoke and heat of the chipotle pepper is a flavor you're never going to get enough of, I promise. The stickiness of this jerky, from the honey, is actually a plus since you have to lick your fingers clean, which makes the great flavor last even longer. By the time you clean your fingers, you're ready for another piece.

INGREDIENTS

½ cup soy sauce

¼ cup honey

1 teaspoon white vinegar

1 teaspoon onion powder

1 teaspoon granulated garlic

1 teaspoon chipotle powder

¼ teaspoon ground black pepper

1 pound London broil strips

INSTRUCTIONS

1. In a 1-gallon resealable plastic freezer bag, thoroughly mix together all the ingredients, except the meat, and allow the mixture to rest for 10 minutes. Add the meat strips to the marinade and mix them around so they get completely coated with the marinade. Remove as much air as possible from the bag, seal, and place it in the refrigerator for 8 to 24 hours. During the marinating time, remove the bag from the refrigerator and work the meat around so the marinade is fully incorporated into it. Remove the strips from the marinade and arrange in a single layer in your choice of dryer. Dry as directed on pages 16–19.

Filet Migjerky

When you go to a steak house, how often do you order the filet mignon? Do you then order a great bottle of red wine to go with it? Then, this jerky is for you. Marinated in a dry red wine with nothing more complicated than salt and pepper, this jerky hits the spot every time. It is a match made in heaven. Sometimes simple really is best.

INGREDIENTS

1 cup dry red wine (Nebbiolo, cabernet, zinfandel)

1 tablespoon Worcestershire sauce

1 teaspoon ground black pepper

1 pound filet mignon, cut into slabs

Maldon sea salt

INSTRUCTIONS

1. In a 1-gallon resealable plastic freezer bag, thoroughly mix together all the ingredients, except the meat and salt, and allow the mixture to rest for 10 minutes. Add the meat slabs to the marinade and mix them around so they get completely coated with the marinade. Remove as much air as possible from the bag, seal, and place it in the refrigerator for 8 to 24 hours. During the marinating time, remove the bag from the refrigerator and work the meat around so the marinade is fully incorporated into it. Remove the slabs from the marinade and arrange in a single layer in your choice of dryer. Sprinkle the meat with sea salt before drying. Dry as directed on pages 16–19.

Spicy Date Jerky

I'm pretty sure the last ingredient you'd think of, when thinking about jerky, is dates. This combo of sweet and spicy is like nothing you've ever had before. The dates make this a pretty sweet jerky but it's rich with lots of exotic flavors . . . and did I mention it's spicy? Put on your big boy/girl pants, cuz this one is *spi-cy*!

INGREDIENTS

2 tablespoons date paste (6 Medjool dates +
    2 tablespoons water, ground together)

2 tablespoons red wine vinegar

2 teaspoons paprika

1 teaspoon chipotle powder

1 teaspoon ancho chile powder

1 teaspoon onion powder

1 teaspoon kosher salt

½ teaspoon dried oregano

½ teaspoon cayenne pepper

¼ teaspoon ground white pepper

¼ teaspoon ground cumin

1 pound London broil strips

INSTRUCTIONS

1. In a 1-gallon resealable plastic freezer bag, thoroughly mix together all the ingredients, except the meat, and allow the mixture to rest for 10 minutes. Add the meat strips to the paste and mix them around so they get completely coated with the marinade. Remove as much air as possible from the bag, seal, and place it in the refrigerator for 8 to 24 hours. During the marinating time, remove the bag from the refrigerator and work the meat around so the paste is fully incorporated into it. Remove the strips from the paste and arrange in a single layer in your choice of dryer. Dry as directed on pages 16–19.

Classic BBQ Jerky

Sometimes you don't want fancy, you just want a classic. This classic BBQ jerky is just that, plain ol' BBQ flavors, with a hint of spice, and lots of meat. When you're looking for familiar flavors, this is what you're going for.

INGREDIENTS

2 tablespoons red currant jelly

1 tablespoon brown sugar

1 tablespoon garlic powder

1 tablespoon onion powder

1 tablespoon ground black pepper

2 teaspoons dried thyme

2 teaspoons smoked paprika

2 teaspoons paprika

½ teaspoon cayenne pepper

½ teaspoon salt

¼ teaspoon ground cloves

1 pound London broil strips

INSTRUCTIONS

1. In a 1-gallon resealable plastic freezer bag, thoroughly mix together all the ingredients, except the meat, and allow the mixture to rest for 10 minutes. Add the meat strips to the paste and mix them around so they get completely coated with the paste. Remove as much air as possible from the bag, seal, and place it in the refrigerator for 8 to 24 hours. During the marinating time, remove the bag from the refrigerator and work the meat around so the paste is fully incorporated into it. Remove the strips from the paste and arrange in a single layer in your choice of dryer. Dry as directed on pages 16–19.

New Mexico Chile Jerky

There's a chile out there known as Hatch. It may look like other chiles, but to be called a Hatch chile, it can only come from Hatch, New Mexico. These chiles run from mild to hot, so the amount of heat in your recipe will be determined by which type of Hatch chile you use. I prefer to use the mild Hatch for this recipe because it has such a nice flavor, and I really want to taste it in the jerky. But if you like the heat . . . go for it! This recipe will work with either one. Fresh Hatch chiles are available in August.

INGREDIENTS

¾ cup roasted and chopped Hatch chiles (about 9 peppers)

½ cup soy sauce

4 teaspoons lemon juice

2 teaspoons white vinegar

½ teaspoon granulated garlic

½ teaspoon salt

½ teaspoon ground black pepper

1 pound London broil strips

INSTRUCTIONS

1. Toss all the ingredients, except the meat, into a food processor and buzz until everything is pureed. Pour the puree into a 1-gallon resealable plastic freezer bag and allow the mixture to rest for 10 minutes. Add the meat strips to the marinade and mix them around so they get completely coated with the marinade. Remove as much air as possible from the bag, seal, and place it in the refrigerator for 8 to 24 hours. During the marinating time, remove the bag from the refrigerator and work the meat around so the marinade is fully incorporated into it. Remove the strips from the marinade and arrange in a single layer in your choice of dryer. Dry as directed on pages 16–19.

Spicy Thai Coconut Ginger Jerky

If you like Thai food, you've found your jerky with this one. It's sticky, sweet, and a whole lot of flavorful. This is my favorite jerky! You can really taste the coconut in this, because it's in here in two different ways, but there's also a bit of heat, too. Even though the coconut milk is unsweetened, the slightly sweet shredded coconut adds a hint of sweetness to the overall flavor. All the flavors in this one are mild, but you can taste each and every one of them. This is another one of those "sticky" jerkies, so there will be lots of finger licking going on.

INGREDIENTS

¾ cup canned coconut milk (not the stuff you find in the liquor aisle)

½ cup soy sauce

⅓ cup sweetened shredded coconut

1 jalapeño pepper, chopped finely

1 tablespoon brown sugar

1 tablespoon grated fresh ginger

1 pound London broil strips

INSTRUCTIONS

1. In a 1-gallon resealable plastic freezer bag, thoroughly mix together all the ingredients, except the meat, and allow the mixture to rest for 10 minutes. Add the meat strips to the marinade and mix them around so they get completely coated with the marinade. Remove as much air as possible from the bag, seal, and place it in the refrigerator for 8 to 24 hours. During the marinating time, remove the bag from the refrigerator and work the meat around so the marinade is fully incorporated into it. Remove the strips from the marinade and arrange in a single layer in your choice of dryer. Dry as directed on pages 16–19.

Chili con Queso Jerky

Traditional chile con queso has nothing to do with meat (notice the e in *chile*). It is a steaming hot bowl of melted cheese with seasonings and some kind of chile. We uninformed people think of it as a steaming hot bowl of meat chili that includes a boatload of Cheddar cheese, but that's chili (with an *i*) con queso. Eating a single piece of this jerky will make you think you've spooned into a rich pot of chili minus the steaming hot temperature. All you need now is a beer and some tortilla chips.

INGREDIENTS

3 tablespoons Cheddar cheese powder

1 tablespoon kosher salt

1 tablespoon tomato powder

1 tablespoon paprika

2 teaspoons ancho chili powder

2 teaspoons granulated garlic

2 teaspoons smoked paprika

1 teaspoon dried Mexican oregano

1 teaspoon ground cumin

1 teaspoon onion powder

½ teaspoon ground black pepper

1 pound London broil strips

INSTRUCTIONS

1. In a small bowl, thoroughly mix together all the ingredients, except the meat. Place the meat strips in a 1-gallon resealable plastic freezer bag and add the dry rub. Mix the strips around so the meat gets completely coated with the dry rub. Remove as much air as possible from the bag, seal, and place it in the refrigerator for 8 to 24 hours. During the marinating time, remove the bag from the refrigerator and work the meat around so the rub is fully incorporated into it. Remove the strips from the rub and arrange in a single layer in your choice of dryer. Dry as directed on pages 16-19.

Root Beer Jerky

Yep, root beer isn't just for turning into ice-cream floats. This jerky has lots of savory flavor to it with only a hint of the sweet root beer on its finish (you won't think you're eating a solid version of root beer soda or sucking on one of those root beer barrel candies). The root beer gives this jerky a really rich flavor and there's just the tiniest bit of chipotle heat. I can't promise that you won't be craving a float when you finish eating all of this root beer jerky, though.

INGREDIENTS

3 cups root beer

⅓ cup soy sauce

1 teaspoon chipotle powder

1 teaspoon paprika

1 teaspoon granulated garlic

¼ teaspoon liquid hickory smoke

1 pound London broil strips

INSTRUCTIONS

1. Mix all the ingredients, except the meat, into a saucepan and heat over medium-high heat. Cook until the mixture reduces by half, 15 to 20 minutes. Remove from the heat and let cool completely. Pour the marinade into a 1-gallon resealable plastic freezer bag and add the meat strips to the marinade. Mix the strips around so they get completely coated with the marinade. Remove as much air as possible from the bag, seal, and place it in the refrigerator for 4 hours. During the marinating time, remove the bag from the refrigerator and work the meat around so the marinade is fully incorporated into it. Remove the strips from the marinade and arrange in a single layer in your choice of dryer. Dry as directed on pages 16-19.

Dr Pepper Jerky

Living in Texas, I thought it was my obligation to make a jerky from one of the state's very popular exports: Dr Pepper. I've always been a big fan of the unique-tasting soda, so it really was a no-brainer to make a beef jerky with it. This jerky gets a sweetness from the soda, with a very subtle Dr Pepper flavor. The soda is a great flavor pairing with beef. No, you won't feel as if you're having a Dr Pepper with a burger; this combination of flavors is really delicious.

INGREDIENTS

2 cups Dr Pepper

1 teaspoon salt

½ teaspoon ground black pepper

½ teaspoon onion powder

½ teaspoon garlic powder

1 pound London broil strips

INSTRUCTIONS

1. Mix all the ingredients, except the meat, in a saucepan and heat over medium-high heat. Cook until the mixture reduces by half, 15 to 20 minutes. Remove from the heat and let cool completely. Pour the marinade into a 1-gallon resealable plastic freezer bag and add the meat strips to the marinade. Mix the strips around so they get completely coated with the marinade. Remove as much air as possible from the bag, seal, and place it in the refrigerator for 4 hours. During the marinating time, remove the bag from the refrigerator and work the meat around so the marinade is fully incorporated into it. Remove the strips from the marinade and arrange in a single layer in your choice of dryer. Dry as directed on pages 16–19.

Chimichurri Beef Jerky

Chimichurri sauce is an Argentinean green sauce that gives beef a tangy taste of vinegar along with an herbal freshness. This chimichurri sauce gets its big flavor from parsley, red onion, and red wine vinegar. It gives your jerky a lighter flavor than is usual, but its tangy deliciousness is unforgettable.

INGREDIENTS

Large handful of flat-leaf parsley

½ small red onion, roughly chopped

2 garlic cloves, roughly chopped

⅓ cup red wine vinegar

1 tablespoon kosher salt

½ teaspoon ground black pepper

½ teaspoon ground cumin

½ teaspoon red pepper flakes

1 pound London broil strips

INSTRUCTIONS

1. Toss all the ingredients, except the meat, into a food processor and buzz until everything is pureed. Pour the puree into a 1-gallon resealable plastic freezer bag and allow the mixture to rest for 10 minutes. Add the meat strips to the marinade and mix them around so they get completely coated with the marinade. Remove as much air as possible from the bag, seal, and place it in the refrigerator for 8 to 24 hours. During the marinating time, remove the bag from the refrigerator and work the meat around so the marinade is fully incorporated into it. Remove the strips from the marinade and arrange in a single layer in your choice of dryer. Dry as directed on pages 16–19.

Sweet Onion Teriyaki Jerky

There's teriyaki and then there's sweet onion teriyaki. In a previous recipe I extolled the virtues of making your own teriyaki sauce because it tastes better; in this recipe we're going to doctor up the bottled stuff. Sweet onions play really nicely with teriyaki sauce and you'll find that this jerky has a great flavor of teriyaki and onion, but neither overwhelms the other. I think you'll start "fixing" up your bottled teriyaki sauce for more than just this jerky recipe after you taste it.

INGREDIENTS

1 (10-ounce) bottle teriyaki sauce (the watery kind)

½ large sweet onion (Maui, Texas, or Walla Walla), roughly chopped

¼ teaspoon liquid hickory smoke

¼ teaspoon ground black pepper

1 pound London broil strips

INSTRUCTIONS

1. Toss all the ingredients, except the meat, into a food processor and buzz until everything is pureed. Pour the puree into a 1-gallon resealable plastic freezer bag and allow the mixture to rest for 10 minutes. Add the meat strips to the marinade and mix the strips around so they get completely coated with the marinade. Remove as much air as possible from the bag, seal, and place it in the refrigerator for 8 to 24 hours. During the marinating time, remove the bag from the refrigerator and work the meat around so the marinade is fully incorporated into it. Remove the strips from the marinade and arrange in a single layer in your choice of dryer. Dry as directed on pages 16–19.

South of the Border Jerky

You have to be careful when using citrus fruit in your meat marinades. Citrus breaks down meat fibers and you can end up with a pile of gray mush, instead of jerky meat. To get just the right South of the Border flavors, I use citric acid powder in place of lime juice. Because you would need so much lime juice to get the flavor you want, marinating the meat overnight in it, using juice would be a bit of a disaster. The citric acid gives you just the right amount of tanginess for the South of the Border jerky taste you're looking for and allows for a longer marinating time. You can find citric acid in regular grocery stores and online. Now break out the tequila and mescal!

INGREDIENTS

½ cup brown sugar

2 teaspoons ground cumin

2 teaspoons ground coriander

2 teaspoons kosher salt

1 teaspoon ancho chile powder

1 teaspoon chipotle powder

1 teaspoon citric acid

1 teaspoon paprika

½ teaspoon cayenne pepper

1 pound London broil strips

INSTRUCTIONS

1. In a small bowl, thoroughly mix together all the ingredients, except the meat. Place the meat strips in a 1-gallon resealable plastic freezer bag and add the dry rub. Mix the strips around so the meat gets completely coated with the dry rub. Remove as much air as possible from the bag, seal, and place it in the refrigerator for 8 to 24 hours. During the marinating time, remove the bag from the refrigerator and work the meat around so the rub is fully incorporated into it. Remove the strips from the rub and arrange in a single layer in your choice of dryer. Dry as directed on pages 16–19.

Jerky au Poivre

When you're at a steak house and you order steak au poivre, what gets presented to you is a steak coated in a rich peppercorn sauce (besides whiskey, pepper is another of steak's best friends). This jerky is just that minus the sauce part, loaded with cracked black pepper. You'll definitely feed your craving for a steak house flavor in an easy-to-carry form.

INGREDIENTS

½ cup soy sauce

1½ tablespoons freshly cracked black pepper

1 tablespoon Worcestershire sauce

1 teaspoon salt

½ teaspoon onion powder

½ teaspoon garlic powder

4 drops liquid hickory smoke

1½ pounds eye of round, cut into strips

INSTRUCTIONS

1. In a 1-gallon resealable plastic freezer bag, thoroughly mix together all the ingredients, except the meat, and allow the mixture to rest for 10 minutes. Add the meat strips to the marinade and mix them around so they get completely coated with the marinade. Remove as much air as possible from the bag, seal, and place it in the refrigerator for 8 to 24 hours. During the marinating time, remove the bag from the refrigerator and work the meat around so the marinade is fully incorporated into it. Remove the strips from the marinade and arrange in a single layer in your choice of dryer. Dry as directed on pages 16–19.

Sweet Tart Jerky

This one took me forever to get right. It either came out too sweet, too tart, or neither. While my neighbors loved getting all the free jerky, I sat in frustration trying to figure this one out. I finally figured it out and you probably already have these ingredients in your kitchen. The tartness is very subtle and just comes through while you're chewing it and the honey gives it a nice soft, sweet flavor. Don't expect this to taste like a meat version of the candy with this same name; these flavors are a whole lot softer.

INGREDIENTS

¼ cup soy sauce

¼ cup unseasoned rice vinegar

¼ cup honey

2 tablespoons ketchup

1 tablespoon sriracha sauce

1 pound London broil strips

INSTRUCTIONS

1. In a 1-gallon resealable plastic freezer bag, thoroughly mix together all the ingredients, except the meat, and allow the mixture to rest for 10 minutes. Add the meat strips to the marinade and mix them around so they get completely coated with the marinade. Remove as much air as possible from the bag, seal, and place it in the refrigerator for 8 to 24 hours. During the marinating time, remove the bag from the refrigerator and work the meat around so the marinade is fully incorporated into it. Remove the strips from the marinade and arrange in a single layer in your choice of dryer. Dry as directed on pages 16-19.

Chile, Lime, and Lager Jerky

Chile and lime has been a popular flavor combination for years; recently it's been showing up with the additional ingredient of beer and I'm not complaining. This flavor combo works great as a marinade for jerky. Just remember . . . beer is a tenderizer and citrus breaks down meat, so this one doesn't swim in the marinade for long or you'll end up with mush. Trust me, it's not pretty and it doesn't taste as good when it's mushy. Set your alarm so you don't forget your meat.

INGREDIENTS

24 ounces lager

½ cup lime juice

⅓ cup soy sauce

2 serrano chiles, cut into large pieces

1 teaspoon granulated garlic

½ teaspoon ground black pepper

1 pound London broil strips

INSTRUCTIONS

1. Toss all the ingredients, except the meat, into a food processor and buzz until everything is pureed. Pour the puree into a 1-gallon resealable plastic freezer bag and allow the mixture to rest for 10 minutes. Add the meat strips to the marinade and mix the strips around so they get completely coated with the marinade. Remove as much air as possible from the bag, seal, and place it in the refrigerator for 4 hours. During the marinating time, remove the bag from the refrigerator and work the meat around so the marinade is fully incorporated into it. Remove the strips from the marinade and arrange in a single layer in your choice of dryer. Dry as directed on pages 16–19.

Cajun Jerky

How could I not include a Cajun-flavored jerky? I kept it extra simple and just used my favorite store-bought brand of seasoning to make up a marinade. Yes, this one is good and spicy (as all good Cajun food should be), so it's not for the faint of heart, or taste buds. You might end up clutching your pearls when eating this one.

INGREDIENTS

2 tablespoons + 2 teaspoons Cajun seasoning (I use Tony Chachere's)

2 tablespoons soy sauce

1 tablespoon brown sugar

1 tablespoon Worcestershire sauce

1½ teaspoons ground black pepper

2 drops liquid hickory smoke

1 pound London broil strips

INSTRUCTIONS

1. In a 1-gallon resealable plastic freezer bag, thoroughly mix together all the ingredients, except the meat, and allow the mixture to rest for 10 minutes. Add the meat strips to the paste and mix them around so they get completely coated with the marinade. Remove as much air as possible from the bag, seal, and place it in the refrigerator for 8 to 24 hours. During the marinating time, remove the bag from the refrigerator and work the meat around so the paste is fully incorporated into it. Remove the strips from the paste and arrange in a single layer in your choice of dryer. Dry as directed on pages 16–19.

Smokehouse Jerky

This is another recipe that took me some time to get just right.
The thing I really like about this jerky is that it doesn't just taste like a big hunk of smoke. Because of the different smoky ingredients, it actually has different smoky flavors in it. You've got the smoke flavor from the mezcal, the smokiness from the smoked paprika, and of course the liquid smoke. All of these add up to different layers of smoke and flavor. Oh, and this jerky isn't spicy. It's all about the smoke.

INGREDIENTS

1 jalapeño pepper, stemmed and roughly chopped

1 large tomato, quartered

1 small lime, skin and pith cut off

1 medium-size onion, roughly chopped

2 garlic cloves

5 teaspoons liquid hickory smoke

1 tablespoon cider vinegar

2 teaspoons mezcal

1 teaspoon chipotle powder

1½ teaspoons salt

1 teaspoon ancho chile powder

1 teaspoon smoked paprika

1 teaspoon dried oregano

½ teaspoon ground black pepper

½ teaspoon ground cumin

1 to 1½ pounds London broil strips

INSTRUCTIONS

1. Toss all the ingredients, except the meat, into a food processor and buzz until everything is pureed. Pour the puree into a 1-gallon resealable plastic freezer bag and allow the mixture to rest for 10 minutes. Add the meat strips to the marinade and mix them around so they get completely coated with the marinade. Remove as much air as possible from the bag, seal, and place it in the refrigerator for 8 to 24 hours. During the marinating time, remove the bag from the refrigerator and work the meat around so the marinade is fully incorporated into it. Remove the strips from the marinade and arrange in a single layer in your choice of dryer. Dry as directed on pages 16–19.

Curry Beef Jerky

Here's another international cuisine that works great in jerky form. The heat or sweet flavor of this jerky depends on the type of curry powder you use. I like a sweeter curry powder, so my version doesn't really have any spice to speak of. If you like hot curry, then use your favorite hot curry powder. This is also a "wet" or slightly sticky jerky because of the coconut milk in the recipe. So when it's dried, the surface will still look a bit shiny.

INGREDIENTS

½ large onion, roughly chopped

2 garlic cloves, smashed

¾ cup canned coconut milk
(not the stuff from the liquor aisle)

¼ cup soy sauce

2 tablespoons brown sugar

2 tablespoons lime juice

4 teaspoons curry powder

1 tablespoon granulated ginger

⅛ teaspoon cayenne pepper

1 pound London broil strips

INSTRUCTIONS

1. Toss all the ingredients, except the meat, into a food processor and buzz until everything is pureed. Pour the puree into a 1-gallon resealable plastic freezer bag and allow the mixture to rest for 10 minutes. Add the meat strips to the marinade and mix them around so they get completely coated with the marinade. Remove as much air as possible from the bag, seal, and place it in the refrigerator for 8 to 24 hours. During the marinating time, remove the bag from the refrigerator and work the meat around so the marinade is fully incorporated into it. Remove the strips from the marinade and arrange in a single layer in your choice of dryer. Dry as directed on pages 16–19.

Spicy Mint Beef Jerky

This Thai-inspired jerky is another one of my favorites. There is so much flavor going on in this jerky, your taste buds will go crazy. I'm salivating just thinking about this one. Pretty much every flavor profile you can think of is in here: sweet, heat, herbal, tart, and of course that magical umami. Once you make this jerky, I dare you to pace yourself eating it. I'm guessing you won't be able to stop yourself from eating the whole bag. Better just make a double batch.

INGREDIENTS

3 garlic cloves

4 dried Thai bird chiles, broken up

2 tablespoons Asian fish sauce (Nam pla or Nuoc Nam)

2 tablespoons soy sauce

1 teaspoon red pepper flakes

2 teaspoons dried basil

1 cup packed fresh mint leaves

2 teaspoons brown sugar

½ large onion, roughly chopped

1 small lime, skin and pith cut off

1 pound London broil strips

INSTRUCTIONS

1. Toss all the ingredients, except the meat, into a food processor and buzz until everything is pureed. Pour the puree into a 1-gallon resealable plastic freezer bag and allow the mixture to rest for 10 minutes. Add the meat strips to the marinade and mix them around so they get completely coated with the marinade. Remove as much air as possible from the bag, seal, and place it in the refrigerator for 8 to 24 hours. During the marinating time, remove the bag from the refrigerator and work the meat around so the marinade is fully incorporated into it. Remove the strips from the marinade and arrange in a single layer in your choice of dryer. Dry as directed on pages 16–19.

Salsa Savvy Jerky

Like salsa? Can't eat a taco or burrito without the stuff? Then, you're going to love this jerky. This recipe uses your favorite salsa for your jerky marinade (there are a couple more ingredients but literally it's two more ingredients). Your favorite salsa is the star of this show.

INGREDIENTS

1½ cups of your favorite salsa

1 teaspoon Maggi seasoning (with the yellow top) or Worcestershire sauce

10 drops liquid hickory smoke

1 pound London broil strips

INSTRUCTIONS

1. In a 1-gallon resealable plastic freezer bag, thoroughly mix together all the ingredients, except the meat, and allow the mixture to rest for 10 minutes. Add the meat strips to the marinade and mix them around so they get completely coated with the marinade. Remove as much air as possible from the bag, seal, and place it in the refrigerator for 8 to 24 hours. During the marinating time, remove the bag from the refrigerator and work the meat around so marinade is fully incorporated into it. Remove the strips from the marinade and arrange in a single layer in your choice of dryer. Dry as directed on pages 16–19.

Asian Kick Jerky

I suppose I could have tried to put more Asian flavors into this jerky, but then you probably wouldn't be able to taste the meat. This isn't a very hot jerky, but it *is* a very flavorful jerky. This is one of those jerkies that I like to keep with me when I'm running all over town trying to get my errands done and I don't want to be tempted to make a run to the drive-through.

INGREDIENTS

¼ cup pineapple juice

2 tablespoons soy sauce

2 tablespoons unseasoned rice vinegar

1 tablespoon sriracha sauce

1 tablespoon sesame oil

1 tablespoon mirin

1 teaspoon red pepper flakes

1 teaspoon grated fresh garlic

1 teaspoon grated fresh ginger

1 pound London broil strips

INSTRUCTIONS

1. In a 1-gallon resealable plastic freezer bag, thoroughly mix together all the ingredients, except the meat, and allow the mixture to rest for 10 minutes. Add the meat strips to the marinade and mix them around so they get completely coated with the marinade. Remove as much air as possible from the bag, seal, and place it in the refrigerator for 8 to 24 hours. During the marinating time, remove the bag from the refrigerator and work the meat around so the marinade is fully incorporated into it. Remove the strips from the marinade and arrange in a single layer in your choice of dryer. Dry as directed on pages 16–19.

Sweet and Spicy Jerky

There was never enough of this jerky to go around when I was testing recipes. Every time I made a batch of this, it was gobbled up in minutes and I had requests for more, more, more. I didn't have too much of a problem fulfilling the requests on this one because it's so easy to whip up. I think this one is so popular is because it's got a great balance of sweet and heat.

INGREDIENTS

½ cup soy sauce

3 tablespoons brown sugar

2½ teaspoons chili oil (with seeds)

5 drops liquid hickory smoke

1 pound sirloin strips

INSTRUCTIONS

1. In a 1-gallon resealable plastic freezer bag, thoroughly mix together all the ingredients, except the meat, and allow the mixture to rest for 10 minutes. Add the meat strips to the marinade and mix them around so they get completely coated with the marinade. Remove as much air as possible from the bag, seal, and place it in the refrigerator for 8 to 24 hours. During the marinating time, remove the bag from the refrigerator and work the meat around so the marinade is fully incorporated into it. Remove the strips from the marinade and arrange in a single layer in your choice of dryer. This one will have a bit longer drying time due to the oil in the recipe. Dry as directed on pages 16–19.

Tailgater Jerky

I grew up in Cleveland, definitely a tailgating town. On those wickedly cold days in the parking lot, we were known to go through cases of beer, pounds of grilled onions, and more hamburgers and hot dogs than I even want to think about now. This jerky takes all of those great flavors and jams every last one of them into a piece of jerky. Of course the twenty-below temperatures are something you'll need Mother Nature for.

INGREDIENTS

12 ounces of your favorite beer (not light beer)

1 large onion, sliced into thin rings

½ cup soy sauce

¼ cup Worcestershire sauce

10 drops liquid hickory smoke

1 pound sirloin strips

INSTRUCTIONS

1. In a 1-gallon resealable plastic freezer bag, thoroughly mix together all the ingredients, except the meat, and allow the mixture to rest for 10 minutes. Add the meat strips to the marinade and mix them around so they get completely coated with the marinade. Remove as much air as possible from the bag, seal, and place it in the refrigerator for 8 to 24 hours. During the marinating time, remove the bag from the refrigerator and work the meat around so the marinade is fully incorporated into it. Remove the strips from the marinade and arrange in a single layer in your choice of dryer. Dry as directed on pages 16–19.

Hot Teriyaki Jerky

Have you noticed how versatile teriyaki is? It's a great sauce that's sweet, salty, and rich tasting all at the same time. That's what makes it perfect to add a few ingredients here and there to tweak it a little bit. This time I added some Chinese hot mustard (for a little sinus-clearing action) along with some crushed red pepper to get the tongue burning a little bit. Oh yeah, I added a little bit more ginger than usual, too, so there's a bit of ginger heat in here. This jerky has lots of layers of flavors and different heat layers. But this isn't a rocket hot jerky, I'd call it moderately hot. Your little sister could eat this one.

INGREDIENTS

¼ cup soy sauce

¼ cup mirin

2 tablespoons sugar

2 tablespoons water

1 tablespoon thinly sliced fresh ginger

1 tablespoon brown sugar

2 garlic cloves, crushed

2½ teaspoons Chinese mustard powder

2 teaspoons red pepper flakes

1 teaspoon lime juice

1 pound London broil strips

INSTRUCTIONS

1. In a 1-gallon resealable plastic freezer bag, thoroughly mix together all the ingredients, except the meat, and allow the mixture to rest for 10 minutes. Add the meat strips to the marinade and mix them around so they get completely coated with the marinade. Remove as much air as possible from the bag, seal, and place it in the refrigerator for 8 to 24 hours. During the marinating time, remove the bag from the refrigerator and work the meat around so the marinade is fully incorporated into it. Remove the strips from the marinade and arrange in a single layer in your choice of dryer. Dry as directed on pages 16–19.

Black and Blue Jerky

If you order a steak in a restaurant as "black and blue," you're going to get a very rare steak on your plate. Around here, black and blue is a steak covered in blue cheese. For the purposes of this book, a black and blue jerky is a great piece of jerky topped with dried blue cheese. Yes, I said blue cheese-topped jerky. I prefer the jerky to be topped with dehydrated blue cheese crumbles, but you can use blue cheese powder instead, if you like.

INGREDIENTS

½ cup soy sauce

¼ cup Worcestershire sauce

2 tablespoons brown sugar

2 teaspoons granulated garlic

1 teaspoon granulated onion

½ teaspoon ground black pepper

Dehydrated or powdered blue cheese (see page 198)

1 pound London broil strips

INSTRUCTIONS

1. In a 1-gallon resealable plastic freezer bag, thoroughly mix together all the ingredients, except the meat and the blue cheese, and allow the mixture to rest for 10 minutes. Add the meat strips to the marinade and mix them around so they get completely coated with the marinade. Remove as much air as possible from the bag, seal, and place it in the refrigerator for 8 to 24 hours. During the marinating time, remove the bag from the refrigerator and work the meat around so the marinade is fully incorporated into it. Remove the strips from the marinade and arrange in a single layer in your choice of dryer. Sprinkle the cheese crumbles or powdered cheese liberally over marinated beef before starting the drying process. Dry as directed on pages 16–19.

Java Jolt Jerky

There's a brand of jerky that pro-
claims it contains caffeine to
help give you a little pick-me-up
during the day. But you can't taste it . . . .
What's the point of that? Coffee and beef work
really well together (hello . . . cowboy steak)
so I wanted to put a little cup of espresso with
your serving of beef. This doesn't taste like
straight-up black coffee with a side of beef,
though. There are other flavors mixed in here to
make the espresso flavor more subtle.

INGREDIENTS

¼ cup molasses

2 tablespoons Worcestershire sauce

1½ tablespoons kosher salt

1 tablespoon espresso powder

1 tablespoon unsweetened cocoa powder

1 teaspoon chili powder

1 teaspoon ground black pepper

½ teaspoon ground cinnamon

1 pound London broil strips

INSTRUCTIONS

1. In a 1-gallon resealable plastic freezer bag, thor-
    oughly mix together all the ingredients, except the
    meat, and allow the mixture to rest for 10 minutes.
    Add the meat strips to the paste and mix them
    around so they get completely coated with the
    marinade. Remove as much air as possible from
    the bag, seal, and place it in the refrigerator for 8
    to 24 hours. During the marinating time, remove
    the bag from the refrigerator and work the meat
    around so the paste is fully incorporated into it.
    Remove the strips from the paste and arrange in a
    single layer in your choice of dryer. Dry as directed
    on pages 16–19.

Smoky Sweet Jerky

A little sweetness, a little smoke, some tang, and a bit of spice complete the flavor profile of this jerky. Inspired by Texas BBQ, which includes all of these things, this jerky will take your taste buds on a little trip to a central Texas smokehouse. But it won't leave you smelling all smoky when you're done.

INGREDIENTS

½ cup soy sauce

2 tablespoons brown sugar

1 tablespoon sugar

1 tablespoon pure maple syrup (grade B)

2 teaspoons liquid hickory smoke

2 teaspoons smoked paprika

2 teaspoons Worcestershire sauce

1 teaspoon dry mustard

½ teaspoon chipotle powder

½ teaspoon ground cinnamon

½ teaspoon ground black pepper

1 pound London broil strips

INSTRUCTIONS

1. In a 1-gallon resealable plastic freezer bag, thoroughly mix together all the ingredients, except the meat, and allow the mixture to rest for 10 minutes. Add the meat strips to the marinade and mix them around so they get completely coated with the marinade. Remove as much air as possible from the bag, seal, and place it in the refrigerator for 8 to 24 hours. During the marinating time, remove the bag from the refrigerator and work the meat around so the marinade is fully incorporated into it. Remove the strips from the marinade and arrange in a single layer in your choice of dryer. Dry as directed on pages 16–19.

Chile Garlic Jerky

Chile garlic sauce is a great condiment to put on practically everything, and here you're making your own. It's got a raw chile and garlic flavor that enhances the flavor of so many things I thought I would test it out on just plain meat. Yep, it makes that taste better, too. As simple as the mixture is, there are lots of complex flavors working to make it taste like a really complicated, yet super delicious jerky.

INGREDIENTS

½ cup soy sauce

¼ cup Worcestershire sauce

2 tablespoons brown sugar

1½ tablespoons chili oil (the kind with the seeds in it)

6 garlic cloves, grated

½ teaspoon ground black pepper

1 pound London broil strips

INSTRUCTIONS

1. In a 1-gallon resealable plastic freezer bag, thoroughly mix together all the ingredients, except the meat, and allow the mixture to rest for 10 minutes. Add the meat strips to the marinade and mix them around so they get completely coated with the marinade. Remove as much air as possible from the bag, seal, and place it in the refrigerator for 8 to 24 hours. During the marinating time, remove the bag from the refrigerator and work the meat around so the marinade is fully incorporated into it. Remove the strips from the marinade and arrange in a single layer in your choice of dryer. Dry as directed on pages 16–19.

Ancho Chile Raspberry Jerky

Ancho chiles deserve as much love, or more, than chipotle. Their sweet and smoky flavor adds a lot of depth to recipes and I think they get the redheaded stepchild treatment a little too much. The smokiness of the ancho chiles is tempered by the sweetness of raspberries in this jerky. While there are plenty of the berries in this recipe, the flavor comes out very subtly. I toned down the sweetness of this jerky by using fresh fruit instead of raspberry jam. If you want some heat in this one, toss in some red pepper flakes.

INGREDIENTS

1 heaping cup raspberries

½ cup soy sauce

¼ cup honey

1 teaspoon balsamic vinegar

1 teaspoon onion powder

1 teaspoon granulated garlic

1 teaspoon ancho chile powder

¼ teaspoon ground black pepper

1 pound London broil strips

INSTRUCTIONS

1. Toss all the ingredients, except the meat, into a food processor and buzz until everything is pureed. Pour the puree into a 1-gallon resealable plastic freezer bag and allow the mixture to rest for 10 minutes. Add the meat strips to the marinade and mix them around so they get completely coated with the marinade. If the seeds really bother you, you can strain the marinade before putting it into the bag with the meat. Remove as much air as possible from the bag, seal, and place it in the refrigerator for 8 to 24 hours. During the marinating time, remove the bag from the refrigerator and work the meat around so the marinade is fully incorporated into it. Remove the strips from the marinade and arrange in a single layer in your choice of dryer. Dry as directed on pages 16–19.

Hot Hickory Jerky

This has also been a very popular flavor among jerky eaters. The trio of peppers gives this jerky a *lot* of flavor. Not only do you get the heat from the peppers, but the smokiness they possess comes through as well. And so nothing in the jerky-making process is wasted, some of the peppers' soaking water gets put back into the marinade, further strengthening the smoky pepper flavors.

INGREDIENTS

3 dried guajillo peppers

3 dried chipotle peppers

1 fresh habanero pepper

½ cup soy sauce

¼ cup Worcestershire sauce

¼ cup pepper-soaking water

2 tablespoons brown sugar

1 tablespoon liquid hickory smoke

2 teaspoons lemon juice

1 teaspoon ground black pepper

1 garlic clove

1 pound top round strips

INSTRUCTIONS

1. Remove the tops from the peppers. Tear the peppers into pieces and drop the pieces into a large bowl. Heat 3 cups of water to a boil and pour over the dried peppers. Let sit for 20 to 40 minutes, or until the peppers are good and soft. Strain the peppers from the water, but make sure to reserve ¼ cup of their soaking water. Toss all the ingredients, except the meat, into a food processor and buzz until everything is pureed. Pour the puree into a 1-gallon resealable plastic freezer bag and allow the mixture to rest for 10 minutes. Add the meat strips to the marinade and mix them around so they get completely coated with the marinade. Remove as much air as possible from the bag, seal, and place it in the refrigerator for 8 to 24 hours. During the marinating time, remove the bag from the refrigerator and work the meat around so the marinade is fully incorporated into it. Remove the strips from the marinade and arrange in a single layer in your choice of dryer. Dry as directed on pages 16–19.

Beef Tamale Jerky

The first company I worked for in Los Angeles had a giant warehouse attached to it. Every year, at Christmas, one of the guys would make his *abuela*'s (grandma's) beef tamale recipe and bring in pans of them for the entire place. For a Cleveland girl, this was some newfound flavors: spicy chile, beef, and masa. I was hooked. This recipe tastes like a dried version of the inside of those beef tamales I enjoyed so many years ago. While it's not insanely hot like those were, there is a bit of heat and loads of great flavor.

INGREDIENTS

4 ounces dried New Mexico (or Hatch) chiles

3 cups water

1½ cups pepper-soaking water

¼ cup Worcestershire sauce

1 medium-size onion, roughly chopped

6 garlic cloves, smashed

3 fresh pasilla chiles, stemmed and peeled

2 tablespoons kosher salt

1½ tablespoons lime juice

1 tablespoon ground cumin

2 teaspoons ancho chile powder

½ teaspoon ground black pepper

2 pounds London broil strips

INSTRUCTIONS

1. Remove the tops from the peppers. Tear the peppers into pieces and drop the pieces into a large bowl. Heat 3 cups of water to a boil and pour over the dried peppers. Let sit for 20 to 40 minutes, or until the peppers are good and soft. Strain the peppers from the water, but make sure to reserve 1½ cups of their soaking water. Toss all the ingredients, except the meat, into a food processor and buzz until everything is pureed. Pour the puree into a 1-gallon resealable plastic freezer bag and allow the mixture to rest for 10 minutes. Add the meat strips to the marinade and mix them around so they get completely coated with the marinade. Remove as much air as possible from the bag, seal, and place it in the refrigerator for 8 to 24 hours. During the marinating time, remove the bag from the refrigerator and work the meat around so the marinade is fully incorporated into it. Remove the strips from the marinade and arrange in a single layer in your choice of dryer. Dry as directed on pages 16–19.

Smoky Honey Jerky

This jerky is all about the smoke and honey. Its rich, well-rounded flavors let you taste the smoke, but the hickory and honey blend harmoniously together. Even though there are quite a few ingredients, the flavor is very simple . . . just the way it should be.

INGREDIENTS

½ cup soy sauce

¼ cup honey

⅛ cup Worcestershire sauce

1 tablespoon liquid hickory smoke

1 teaspoon white vinegar

1 teaspoon onion powder

1 teaspoon granulated garlic

½ teaspoon ground black pepper

⅛ teaspoon cayenne pepper

1 pound thin-cut top round beef strips

INSTRUCTIONS

1. In a 1-gallon resealable plastic freezer bag, thoroughly mix together all the ingredients, except the meat, and allow the mixture to rest for 10 minutes. Add the meat strips to the marinade and mix them around so they get completely coated with the marinade. Remove as much air as possible from the bag, seal, and place it in the refrigerator for 8 to 24 hours. During the marinating time, remove the bag from the refrigerator and work the meat around so the marinade is fully incorporated into it. Remove the strips from the marinade and arrange in a single layer in your choice of dryer. Dry as directed on pages 16–19.

Sweet Cajun Onion Jerky

The spicy heat and flavor of Cajun tamed, just a bit, with the sweetness of onion. While it's pretty hard to get an actual sweet Cajun onion, rumored to grow in Louisiana, swapping in a Texas Sweet or Vidalia onion into this jerky recipe works just as well. I love the sweetness that it brings to that Cajun heat. The sweetness calms your tongue just enough to let you eat even more.

INGREDIENTS

1 large sweet onion (Walla Walla, Texas Sweet, or Maui), peeled and quartered

1 garlic clove

¼ cup soy sauce

2 tablespoons Cajun seasoning

2 tablespoons brown sugar

½ teaspoon ground black pepper

¼ teaspoon liquid hickory smoke

1 pound London broil strips

INSTRUCTIONS

1. Toss all the ingredients, except the meat, into a food processor and buzz until everything is pureed. Pour the puree into a 1-gallon resealable plastic freezer bag and allow the mixture to rest for 10 minutes. Add the meat strips to the marinade and mix them around so they get completely coated with the marinade. Remove as much air as possible from the bag, seal, and place it in the refrigerator for 8 to 24 hours. During the marinating time, remove the bag from the refrigerator and work the meat around so the marinade is fully incorporated into it. Remove the strips from the marinade and arrange in a single layer in your choice of dryer. Dry as directed on pages 16–19.

Sweet & Spicy Twist Jerky

This jerky isn't just a combination of sweet and spicy; it's two separate jerkies twisted together—one sweet and one spicy. How twisted! I didn't want to just combine the flavors and have them run together. I wanted each to be its own separate flavor. I know people sometimes like to eat two different flavors at once, and this jerky lets you do it without looking weird. Holding one flavor in each hand is a dead giveaway that's what you're doing, by the way.

INGREDIENTS

THE SWEET SIDE

¼ cup soy sauce

2 tablespoons honey

2 tablespoons brown sugar

1 tablespoon frozen orange juice concentrate

1 teaspoon vanilla extract

½ pound London broil strips

THE SPICY SIDE

⅓ cup bourbon

2 tablespoons kosher salt

2 tablespoons water

1 tablespoon chipotle powder

2 garlic cloves, grated

¼ teaspoon ground black pepper

½ pound London broil strips

INSTRUCTIONS

1. You'll need to follow these directions separately for the sweet and the spicy versions of this jerky. In a 1-gallon resealable plastic freezer bag, thoroughly mix together all the ingredients for each "side," except the meat, and allow the mixture to rest for 10 minutes. Add the meat strips to the marinade and mix them around so they get completely coated with the marinade. Remove as much air as possible from the bag, seal, and place it in the refrigerator for 8 to 24 hours. During the marinating time, remove the bag from the refrigerator and work the meat around so the marinade is fully incorporated into it.

2. When ready to dry, remove one strip from each marinade bag, then twist them together. Continue until all the strips are paired up and twisted. Arrange the twists in a single layer in your choice of dryer. Dry as directed on pages 16–19.

French Onion Beef Jerky

You know those little packets of French onion soup that everyone's mom used when she made meat-loaf and that killer French onion chip dip? You can use those same packets to make an amazingly delicious jerky, too! This is the highly portable version of that snooty French restaurant dish of French onion soup. It's so good, I don't even think you'll miss the gooey cheese and bread on this.

INGREDIENTS

2 (1-ounce) packages French onion soup mix

1 medium-size onion, quartered

2 garlic cloves, roughly chopped

½ cup soy sauce

¼ cup Worcestershire sauce

⅛ teaspoon ground black pepper

1 pound London broil strips

INSTRUCTIONS

1. Toss all the ingredients, except the meat, into a food processor and buzz until everything is pureed. Pour the puree into a 1-gallon resealable plastic freezer bag and allow the mixture to rest for 10 minutes. Add the meat strips to the marinade and mix them around so they get completely coated with the marinade. Remove as much air as possible from the bag, seal, and place it in the refrigerator for 6 to 8 hours. During the marinating time, remove the bag from the refrigerator and work the meat around so the marinade is fully incorporated into it. Remove the strips from the marinade and arrange in a single layer in your choice of dryer. Dry as directed on pages 16–19.

Jerky Chew

Take any jerky recipe that's not sticky, drop it in the food processor, and proceed to pulverize (shred) it, and you've got jerky chew. Some people put a pinch between their cheek and gum (much like chewing tobacco) and some just toss it straight into their mouth and chew. An intense flavor that instantly fills your mouth with flavors of meat and seasonings is what jerky chew is, and it's not for wimps. This is a classic jerky recipe that's full of smoke, black pepper, and rich meat flavors. Get ready for the intensity!

INGREDIENTS

½ cup soy sauce

2 tablespoons Worcestershire sauce

2 tablespoons ground black pepper

½ teaspoon liquid hickory smoke

½ teaspoon granulated garlic

½ teaspoon granulated onion

1 pound London broil strips

INSTRUCTIONS

1. In a 1-gallon resealable plastic freezer bag, thoroughly mix together all the ingredients, except the meat, and allow the mixture to rest for 10 minutes. Add the meat strips to the marinade and mix them around so they get completely coated with the marinade. Remove as much air as possible from the bag, seal, and place it in the refrigerator for 8 to 24 hours. During the marinating time, remove the bag from the refrigerator and work the meat around so the marinade is fully incorporated into it. Remove the strips from the marinade and arrange in a single layer in your choice of dryer. Dry as directed on pages 16–19.

2. Once the jerky has dried and cooled to room temperature, you can pulverize it. Just drop two or three pieces into your food processor at a time. If you add too many, you may burn out your motor (it's really hard on the processor to chew up the jerky). Continue adding jerky until you have the amount of jerky chew that you want. Store the jerky chew in an airtight container.

Chipotle Peach Jerky

You can definitely tell I'm in the South. I've converted to eating smoked and dried meats, saying "puh-cahn" instead of "pee-can" and using peaches in everything. This jerky has a great sweet peach flavor when you first bite into it, followed with a nice bit of smoke and heat. It's a bit sticky from the peach preserves, but that gives you more time to savor the flavor while you lick your fingers clean.

INGREDIENTS

½ cup soy sauce

½ cup peach preserves

2 teaspoons white vinegar

1 teaspoon granulated onion

1 teaspoon granulated garlic

1 teaspoon chipotle powder

1 pound London broil strips

INSTRUCTIONS

1. In a 1-gallon resealable plastic freezer bag, thoroughly mix together all the ingredients, except the meat, and allow the mixture to rest for 10 minutes. Add the meat strips to the marinade and mix them around so they get completely coated with the marinade. Remove as much air as possible from the bag, seal, and place it in the refrigerator for 8 to 24 hours. During the marinating time, remove the bag from the refrigerator and work the meat around so the marinade is fully incorporated into it. Remove the strips from the marinade and arrange in a single layer in your choice of dryer. Dry as directed on pages 16–19.

Corned Beef Jerky

Yes, that dinner you love (and look forward to) every year can be turned into delicious jerky. What does it take? How about just buying your favorite corned beef from your local grocery store? Yep, that's about as hard as it gets . . . taking a drive to the grocery store. I really like this jerky; the only thing missing from it is some cooked cabbage and potatoes.

INGREDIENTS

1 (3- to 4-pound) package corned beef strips

INSTRUCTIONS

1. Remove the seasoning packet (you don't need that). Arrange the strips in a single layer on your choice of dehydrator. You don't need to do any additional seasoning or marinating for this one. There's plenty of salt already in the meat from the corning process. Arrange strips in a single layer in your choice of dryer. Dry as directed on pages 16–19.

Camper Jerky

There's nothing fancy about this jerky at all. It's a great road trip snack. It's easy to eat because it's made with ground beef, so it's not as chewy and more on the crunchy side. The seasonings are also very mild. This ground beef jerky is so easy to make and it turns out better when you make it in the oven than in the dehydrator.

INGREDIENTS

1 pound 90/10 ground beef

¼ cup soy sauce

1 tablespoon Worcestershire sauce

1 teaspoon granulated garlic

1 teaspoon granulated onion

½ teaspoon ground black pepper

⅛ teaspoon cayenne pepper

INSTRUCTIONS

1. In a medium-size bowl, mix all the ingredients together and let sit for 10 minutes. Lay a large piece of parchment paper down and put the meat on top of it. Unroll a large piece of plastic wrap and lay that on top of the meat. Begin to press the meat out with your palms, use a rolling pin to get it to ¼-inch thickness, then remove the plastic wrap. If drying in the oven, slide the meat-covered parchment paper directly onto a baking sheet. Score the meat into rectangular shapes so it's easier to break them apart when done drying. If using a dehydrator, cut the meat into rectangles. Use an offset spatula to arrange the pieces on the fruit roll tray and begin drying as directed on pages 16-19.

Sorta Pemmican

This is not traditional pemmican.

Traditional pemmican is roughly two parts fat to one part meat with dried fruit included. It has always been part of the indigenous diet. Yes, this runs counterintuitive to traditional jerky making, but true pemmican isn't really jerky; it uses jerky as one of its ingredients. I know the hardcore Paleo people are into true pemmican, but to the traditional palate, the real thing is hard to swallow (literally). This is a take on pemmican in that it includes meat and dried fruit, but it does not add fat to the mixture. Sorry, guys and girls! But this is pretty darn delicious and great to take along on a hike or camping trip.

INGREDIENTS

- 1 pound 90/10 ground beef
- ½ cup dried cranberries
- ½ cup dried blueberries
- 2 tablespoons soy sauce
- 1 tablespoon Worcestershire sauce
- 1 tablespoon brown sugar
- 1 teaspoon kosher salt
- 1 teaspoon granulated garlic
- 1 teaspoon granulated onion
- ½ teaspoon ground black pepper

INSTRUCTIONS

1. In a medium-size bowl, mix all the ingredients together and let sit for 10 minutes. Lay a large piece of parchment paper down and put the meat on top of it. Unroll a large piece of plastic wrap and lay that on top of the meat. Begin to press the meat out with your palms, use a rolling pin to get it to ¼-inch thickness, then remove the plastic wrap. If drying in the oven, slide the meat-covered parchment paper directly on to baking sheet. Score the meat into rectangular shapes so it's easier to break them apart when done drying. If using a dehydrator, cut the meat into rectangles. Use an offset spatula to arrange the pieces on the fruit roll tray and begin drying as directed on pages 16–19.

Barbacoa Jerky

This is a jerkified version of
a traditional *barbacoa* recipe.

Because using the traditional cheek or head meat wouldn't work for jerky (too fatty), this one is made from ground beef. It gives you a good bit of heat in the back of your throat that gets stronger the more you eat. But there are lots of different flavors in this jerky. This is a great backpacker/road trip/camping jerky and it's not too salty, either.

INGREDIENTS

1 pound 90/10 ground beef

1 tablespoon Worcestershire sauce

1 tablespoon hot Hatch chile powder

1 tablespoon kosher salt, plus more for sprinkling

2 teaspoons tomato powder

1 teaspoon dried oregano

1 teaspoon granulated garlic

1 teaspoon granulated onion

1 teaspoon dried oregano

1 teaspoon paprika

½ teaspoon ground black pepper

½ teaspoon ground cumin

INSTRUCTIONS

1. In a medium-size bowl, mix all the ingredients together and let sit for 10 minutes. Lay a large piece of parchment paper down and put the meat on top of it. Unroll a large piece of plastic wrap and lay that on top of the meat. Begin to press the meat out with your palms, use a rolling pin to get it to ¼-inch thickness, then remove the plastic wrap. If drying in the oven, slide the meat-covered parchment paper directly on to a baking sheet. Score the meat into rectangular shapes so it's easier to break them apart when done drying. If using a dehydrator, cut the meat into rectangles. Use an offset spatula to arrange the pieces on the fruit roll tray and begin drying as directed on pages 16–19. Before drying in either the oven or the dehydrator, sprinkle the top of the meat with a bit more kosher salt.

CHAPTER 3

Pork and Lamb

While they might not be the first types of jerky that come to mind, pork and lamb make for some pretty tasty jerky. While lamb can sometimes take on a "gamey" flavor, once you add the marinades and spices then dehydrate it, that gaminess is practically non-existent. That means that even though you swear you don't like lamb, I'll bet you like these lamb jerky recipes a lot!

Pork is another jerky meat that works really well. Its light flavor lets those marinades and seasonings really shine. I had lots of international influences when I was making the pork jerky, but one that I just couldn't leave out was the Pig Candy. I know it's technically not jerky, but how could I not share this addicting treat with you?

A few tips to make your jerky-making life easier:

- Wear gloves when you're working with raw pork. Wearing the gloves will help cut down on cross contamination. It's also important that everything you use on the pork is very clean. You can't be too clean when it comes to working with raw meat.

- Buying lamb tenderloin is the best cut of meat to use when making lamb jerky. There's no de-boning or skinning. Partially freezing the lamb loin (for about 45 minutes) will help to make cutting the ⅛"–¼" slices easier. (No

defrosting already frozen lamb tenderloin in the microwave though.)

- Buying pork tenderloin is the best cut of meat to use when making pork jerky. There's no de-boning, skinning or even pre-freezing necessary. Because these are so thick, you can cut them to ⅛"–¼" thick slices pretty easily

without having to freeze them. But you certainly can partially freeze them first if you like. (No defrosting already frozen pork tenderloin in the microwave though.)

Like other meats, both lamb and pork can be cut into slab or strips.

Balsamic Pork Jerky

Even the lowly jerky is going upscale. A lean pork tenderloin is sliced thinly and marinated in a balsamic reduction with herbs overnight, then dried to perfection. The result is a gourmet jerky treat that's sweet, tart, herbal, and next to impossible to stop eating. And you don't even have to dress up and leave the house to eat it.

INGREDIENTS

1 cup balsamic vinegar

¼ cup water

2 (4-inch) sprigs fresh rosemary, bruised

1 teaspoon granulated garlic

½ teaspoon kosher salt

1 pound pork tenderloin, cut into slabs

INSTRUCTIONS

1. Pour the vinegar into a small pan and heat over medium-high heat until it has reduced to ½ cup, about 10 minutes. Let the vinegar cool to room temperature, then proceed. To bruise the rosemary, put the sprigs between your palms and clap or rub hard. In a 1-gallon resealable plastic freezer bag, thoroughly mix together all the ingredients, except the meat, and allow the mixture to rest for 10 minutes. Add the meat slabs to the marinade and mix them around so they get completely coated with the marinade. Remove as much air as possible from the bag, seal, and place it in the refrigerator for 8 to 24 hours. During the marinating time, remove the bag from the refrigerator and work the meat around so the marinade is fully incorporated into it. Remove the slabs from the marinade (discard the rosemary) and arrange in a single layer in your choice of dryer. Dry as directed on pages 16–19.

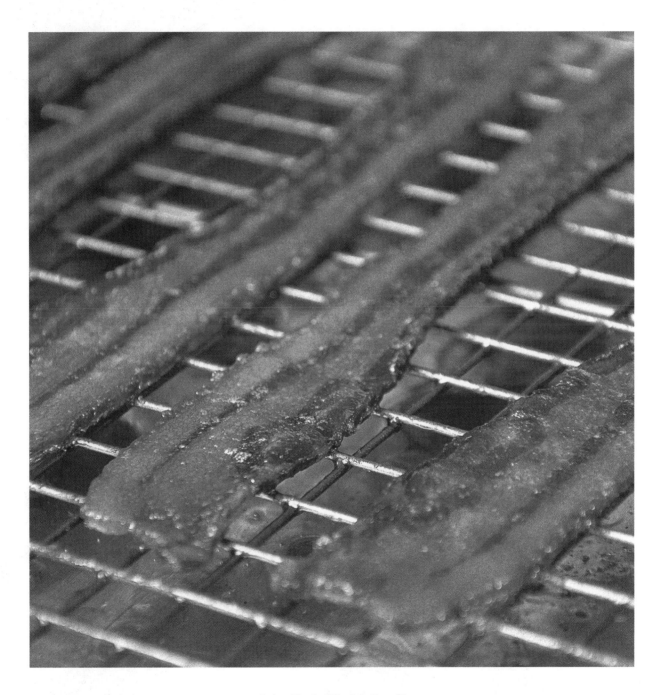

Maple Cayenne Pig Candy

This one technically isn't jerky.
Who cares . . . it tastes *fan-tastic*! Turning actual strips of bacon into jerky isn't really doable for the home jerky maker because there's just too much fat in it, but this is as close as you can get. When you're done making this, you'll have bacon extraordinaire! It's sweet, spicy, smoky, and actually even a bit chewy. It's definitely not crisp and crunchy like regular bacon. You're going to become addicted to this and I'm not sorry for causing the addiction.

INGREDIENTS

½ cup pure maple syrup (grade B)

Cayenne pepper

1 (8 to 12 ounce) package uncured applewood-smoked bacon

INSTRUCTIONS

1. Preheat the oven to 225°F. Line a rimmed baking sheet with aluminum foil and lay a cooling rack on top of the foil (this allows the fat to drip down away from the bacon). Pour the maple syrup into a wide bowl. Dredge the bacon through the maple syrup and arrange in a single layer on the cooling rack. Sprinkle each slice with cayenne. Bake for 3 to 4 hours, turning the bacon slices over every hour. The bacon is done when you bend it and it just starts to crack.

Memphis-Style Jerky

Tennessee is known for its music in Nashville and BBQ in Memphis.

When you hear the phrase "Memphis style," they're talking about Memphis-style BBQ. There are certain states that have a particular "style" of BBQ. It's not just turn on the grill and slap your favorite sauce on the meat. Now that I live in one of those places, I have a better understanding of the beliefs behind the religion. This jerky is of the Memphis style of BBQ, which is a dry rub on pork.

INGREDIENTS

2 tablespoons brown sugar

1½ tablespoons paprika

1 tablespoon salt

1 tablespoon garlic powder

2 teaspoons ground black pepper

2 teaspoons chili powder

1½ teaspoons dried thyme

1 teaspoon dry mustard

½ teaspoon celery seeds

1 pound pork tenderloin strips

INSTRUCTIONS

1. In a bowl, thoroughly mix together all the ingredients, except the meat, and allow the mixture to rest for 10 minutes. Place the meat strips in a 1-gallon resealable plastic freezer bag and add the dry rub. Mix them around so the meat gets completely coated with the dry rub. Remove as much air as possible from the bag, seal, and place it in the refrigerator for 8 to 24 hours. During the marinating time, remove the bag from the refrigerator and work the meat around so the rub is fully incorporated into it. Remove the strips from the rub and arrange in a single layer in your choice of dryer. Dry as directed on pages 16–19.

Bloody Mary Straws

Everybody's adding bacon to everything these days, including cocktails. But the one cocktail where I think it makes the most sense is the Bloody Mary. A piece of crispy, salty bacon jammed into a glass of a savory cocktail? Genius. But why not turn that accoutrement into a functional part of the drink? I give you the Bloody Mary meat straw (dehydrated ham tastes like bacon). While this isn't a perfect straw, you can still get that delicious Bloody Mary through this straw and eat the straw when you're done.

INGREDIENTS

¼ teaspoon celery salt

¼ teaspoon salt

¼ teaspoon paprika

¼ teaspoon onion powder

¼ teaspoon garlic powder

6 slices of deli cooked ham (from the cold cuts section of the grocery store)

INSTRUCTIONS

1. In a small bowl, mix all the ingredients together, except the meat. Arrange the slices of ham in a single layer on a cutting board. Sprinkle the dry mixture evenly over the ham. Roll each ham slice as tightly as you can into a cylinder (with the seasonings on the inside or outside—your choice). Arrange the straws in a single layer on the dryer sheet and dry as directed on pages 16–19.

Bacon Cheddar Pepper Jerky

Believe it or not, there's no bacon or Cheddar cheese in this jerky—but it sure tastes like it. There's a nice heat from the freshly ground black pepper, and the nutritional yeast gives you that great Cheddar flavor. This is a great flavor match for pork.

INGREDIENTS

½ cup liquid aminos

½ cup water

¼ cup liquid hickory smoke

2 tablespoons smoked paprika

4 teaspoons sugar

2½ teaspoons ground black pepper

2 teaspoons granulated onion

2 tablespoons nutritional yeast

1 pound pork sirloin strips

INSTRUCTIONS

1. In a 1-gallon resealable plastic freezer bag, thoroughly mix together all the ingredients, except the meat, and allow the mixture to rest for 10 minutes. Add the meat strips to the marinade and mix them around so they get completely coated with the marinade. Remove as much air as possible from the bag, seal, and place it in the refrigerator for 8 to 24 hours. During the marinating time, remove the bag from the refrigerator and work the meat around the marinade is fully incorporated into it. Remove the strips from the marinade and arrange in a single layer in your choice of dryer. Dry as directed on pages 16–19.

Ka-Pow Jerky

When I let my imagination run wild, things can get a little weird; that's how this recipe came to be. I started thinking about what you would get if you crossed a cow and a pig and what you would call it. Ka-pow! Get it? I know, weird. But this jerky is really pretty tasty. See those stripes? That's pork wrapped around beef. The flavor combination is delicious and all the guys who tried it were asking for more. In fact, I think one of them is trying to figure out if he can get the whole cow/pig combo thing to work out.

INGREDIENTS

3 tablespoons liquid aminos

2 tablespoons pure maple syrup

2 tablespoons cider vinegar

2 tablespoons kosher salt

1 teaspoon paprika

½ teaspoon smoked paprika

½ teaspoon ground black pepper

¼ teaspoon liquid hickory smoke

2 garlic cloves, smashed

1 pound London broil strips

¼ pound deli-sliced Black Forest ham, cut into ¼-inch-wide strips

INSTRUCTIONS

1. In a 1-gallon resealable plastic freezer bag, thoroughly mix together all the ingredients, except the meat, and allow the mixture to rest for 10 minutes. Add the beef strips to the marinade and mix them around so they get completely coated with the marinade. Remove as much air as possible from the bag, seal, and place it in the refrigerator for 8 to 24 hours. During the marinating time, remove the bag from the refrigerator and work the meat around so the marinade is fully incorporated into it. Remove the strips from the marinade and arrange in a single layer in your choice of dryer. As directed on pages 16–19, dry the beef for 1 hour, then wrap the ham strips around the beef strips. Continue the drying process. (The ham does not go in the marinade.)

Char Siu Pork Jerky

This popular Chinese takeout dish gets the jerky treatment.

Although this jerky is a bit sticky, much like the original dish itself, this portable version is a lot easier to eat in the car than trying to maneuver the steering wheel while using chopsticks to eat chunks of pork and rice at the same time as you're balancing a Styrofoam container on your knees.

INGREDIENTS

¼ cup hoisin sauce

¼ cup honey

¼ cup soy sauce

¼ cup rum

1 tablespoon sesame oil

1 teaspoon granulated ginger

1 teaspoon Chinese five-spice powder

1 teaspoon onion powder

1 pound pork tenderloin strips

INSTRUCTIONS

1. In a 1-gallon resealable plastic freezer bag, thoroughly mix together all the ingredients, except the meat, and allow the mixture to rest for 10 minutes. Add the meat strips to the marinade and mix them around so they get completely coated with the marinade. Remove as much air as possible from the bag, seal, and place it in the refrigerator for 8 to 24 hours. During the marinating time, remove the bag from the refrigerator and work the meat around so the marinade is fully incorporated into it. Remove the strips from the marinade and arrange in a single layer in your choice of dryer. Dry as directed on pages 16–19.

Smoky Peachy Piggy Jerky

This sticky little jerky is a crowd favorite! Its slightly sweet yet salty flavors appeal to most everyone and there's a good bit of peach flavor that comes through. In true Southern spirit, a bit of bourbon was added as a great companion to both the peach and pork flavors. Oh, you can taste the bourbon in this, too.

INGREDIENTS

½ cup bourbon

½ cup peach preserves

¼ cup brown sugar

2 tablespoons kosher salt

2 tablespoons cider vinegar

1 tablespoon Worcestershire sauce

2 teaspoons liquid hickory smoke

½ teaspoon ground black pepper

1 pound pork sirloin strips

INSTRUCTIONS

1. Toss all the ingredients, except the meat, into a food processor and buzz until everything is pureed. Pour the puree into a 1-gallon resealable plastic freezer bag and allow the mixture to rest for 10 minutes. Add the meat strips to the marinade and mix them around so they get completely coated with the marinade. Remove as much air as possible from the bag, seal, and place it in the refrigerator for 8 to 24 hours. During the marinating time, remove the bag from the refrigerator and work the meat around so the marinade is fully incorporated into it. Remove the strips from the marinade and arrange in a single layer in your choice of dryer. Dry as directed on pages 16–19.

Jalapeño Maple Bacon Jerky

This jerky mixes our northern Canadian neighbors, bacon and maple syrup, with our southern Mexican neighbors, jalapeños, for a cultural melding of flavors that's delicious. This jerky is so easy to make, since the bacon has already been cut for you. It gets pretty crispy, so it eats more like a chip than a chewy jerky. Make a big batch of this and put it out in a bowl at your next party and you'll be very popular.

INGREDIENTS

2 (6-ounce) packages Canadian bacon

2 medium jalapeño peppers

2 garlic cloves

1 cup pure grade B maple syrup

¼ cup lemon juice

¼ teaspoon ground black pepper

INSTRUCTIONS

1. Toss all the ingredients, except the meat, into a food processor and buzz until everything is pureed. Pour the puree into a 1-gallon resealable plastic freezer bag and allow the mixture to rest for 10 minutes. Add the meat strips to the marinade and mix them around so they get completely coated with the marinade. Remove as much air as possible from the bag, seal, and place it in the refrigerator for 8 to 24 hours. During the marinating time, remove the bag from the refrigerator and work the meat around so the marinade is fully incorporated into it. Remove the strips from the marinade and arrange in a single layer in your choice of dryer. Dry as directed on pages 16–19.

Cuban Pork Jerky

On a trip to Miami several years ago, my friends took me down to Little Havana to experience the culture and the food. I fell in love with the traditional Cuban sandwich. The roasted pork sandwich is simple: roast pork, ham, Swiss cheese, mustard, and pickles, all on chewy Cuban bread and then pressed. This recipe gives you all of that deliciousness in a single piece of jerky, no napkin required.

INGREDIENTS

- 1 cup orange juice
- ⅔ cup lime juice
- 7 garlic cloves, grated
- 4 teaspoons dried oregano leaves
- 2 teaspoons salt
- 1 teaspoon ground cumin
- ½ teaspoon granulated onion
- 1 pound pork tenderloin slices

INSTRUCTIONS

1. In a 1-gallon resealable plastic freezer bag, thoroughly mix together all the ingredients, except the meat, and allow the mixture to rest for 10 minutes. Add the meat strips to the marinade and mix them around so they get completely coated with the marinade. Remove as much air as possible from the bag, seal, and place it in the refrigerator for 4 to 6 hours. During the marinating time, remove the bag from the refrigerator and work the meat around so the marinade is fully incorporated into it. Remove the strips from the marinade and arrange in a single layer in your choice of dryer. Dry as directed on pages 16–19.

Lebanese Lamb Jerky

I'm a big fan of seasoning mixes.
I like the exotic flavors you get when you combine simple herbs and spices together. This lamb jerky is pretty exotic for a jerky recipe. There are so many layers of flavor in there your brain just won't know where to start. If you've been put off lamb before, because of its gaminess, you should really try this jerky. With all of the seasonings in here, you won't get a gamey flavor from the lamb.

INGREDIENTS

    2 teaspoons kosher salt
    1 teaspoon ground cloves
    1 teaspoon ground cumin
    1 teaspoon cinnamon
    1 teaspoon granulated garlic
    ¾ teaspoon paprika
    ¼ teaspoon ground nutmeg
    ¼ teaspoon cayenne pepper
    1 to 1½ pounds lamb loin, cut into slabs

INSTRUCTIONS

1. In a small bowl, thoroughly mix together all the ingredients, except the meat. Place the meat slabs in a 1-gallon resealable plastic freezer bag and add the dry rub. Mix the strips around so the meat gets completely coated with the dry rub. Remove as much air as possible from the bag, seal, and place it in the refrigerator for 8 to 24 hours. During the marinating time, remove the bag from the refrigerator and work the meat around so the rub is fully incorporated into it. Remove the slabs from the rub and arrange in a single layer in your choice of dryer. Dry as directed on pages 16–19.

Rogan Josh Jerky

South of the Border recipes aren't the only flavors that work for jerky; how about some of your favorite Indian dishes? Using lots of spices gives the lamb loads of flavor while helping to eliminate any gaminess that might still be in the lamb meat. You'll find that this one is slightly sweet from the cardamom, cinnamon, and cloves with just a bit of heat that slowly builds with each piece you eat. Just like the dish itself.

INGREDIENTS

1 tablespoon granulated garlic

1 tablespoon paprika

1 teaspoon ground ginger

1 bay leaf, crumbled

½ teaspoon ground coriander

½ teaspoon ground cumin

½ teaspoon onion powder

½ teaspoon cayenne pepper

½ teaspoon salt

½ teaspoon ground black pepper

¼ teaspoon ground cardamom

¼ teaspoon ground cinnamon

⅛ teaspoon ground cloves

1 pound lamb loin strips

INSTRUCTIONS

1. In a small bowl, thoroughly mix together all the ingredients, except the meat. Place the meat strips in a 1-gallon resealable plastic freezer bag and add the dry rub. Mix the strips around so the meat gets completely coated with the dry rub. Remove as much air as possible from the bag, seal, and place it in the refrigerator for 8 to 24 hours. During the marinating time, remove the bag from the refrigerator and work the meat around so the rub is fully incorporated into it. Remove the strips from the rub and arrange in a single layer in your choice of dryer. Dry as directed on pages 16–19.

CHAPTER 4

Game

Game meats are fun to make into jerky. Not that the process is any different, just that the flavors are unique. People who hunt deer usually know all about making jerky, because that's how a lot of it ends up getting eaten. A deer has a lot of lean meat and not everyone is a fan. So what's a hunter to do if he/she doesn't want that meat to go to waste?

The same marinades, dry rubs, and pastes that you use on beef would all work great on game meats. But remember, because the meat itself tastes different, the end product is going to taste different.

A few tips to make your game meat jerky-making life easier:

- Make sure your wild game meat is coming from a reliable source. If an inexperienced hunter field dresses an animal and doesn't do it properly, you could be exposed to some pretty nasty stuff.

- Know your meat. If you want to try making jerky out of bear meat, do a little research on bear meat. Some animals harbor certain types of bacteria and other not so good things, and you need to know how to work with these meats so you can neutralize the problem.

- Remember that this game meat isn't going to taste just like beef or just like chicken … it's going to taste like the animal that it is. That means if you make a game meat jerky with the same marinade as a beef jerky, don't be surprised when the game meat jerky doesn't taste exactly the same.

- It's perfectly fine to make jerky out of a piece of meat that you've had in the freezer for a month

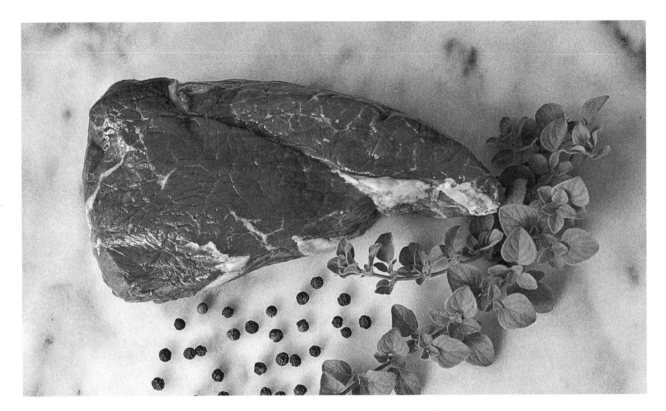

or two. You'll just need to let it thaw a little bit. Don't be concerned by the brown spots you may see on the meat; those happen when meat has been frozen. The meat is fine. Do not thaw the meat in the microwave. A lot of times this causes the meat to actually cook in spots and that will change the consistency of your slabs or strips to be marinated and dried.

- **Electric knives.** Not many people even use these anymore, but they can also be used for cutting jerky. I know I said no serrated knives, earlier, but the electric knife is different.

- **Deli slicer.** If you're fortunate enough to have one of these machines at your disposal, feel free to use that. You'll get beautifully even slices and you'll have an easier time cutting meat for slab jerky.

- Game meats can be cut into slab or strip jerky; the choice is yours. What's the difference between slab vs. strip jerky? Slab jerky is generally cut going with the grain of the meat in thin, wide pieces. Slab jerky is very chewy. Strip jerky is cut against the grain and forms a strip that's only as wide as the meat is high. Strip jerky is tender and easy to chew. Feel free to cut your jerky any way that you like.

Smokin' Hot Bison Jerky

Bison is a lean, rich tasting, red meat that's finally making its way into regular grocery stores, and not just in ground form anymore. Because it's so low in fat, it's perfect for jerky making; you've got to add lots of seasoning to it, though, to make up for the lack of fat flavoring in it. Like its name, this one is smokin' hot. There's a great smokiness to it and the combination of habanero and black pepper is a one-two punch in the hot zone.

INGREDIENTS

½ cup soy sauce

½ cup Worcestershire sauce

1 tablespoon honey

1 tablespoon granulated garlic

2 habanero peppers

2 teaspoons ground black pepper

1½ teaspoons liquid hickory smoke

1 pound bison strips

FOR LESS HEAT MAKE THESE SUBSTITUTIONS . . .

¼ cup soy sauce (instead of ½ cup)

2 teaspoons honey (instead of 1 teaspoon)

2 teaspoons granulated garlic (instead of 1 tablespoon)

1 habanero pepper (instead of 2 peppers)

INSTRUCTIONS

1. Toss all the ingredients, except the meat, into a food processor and buzz until everything is pureed. Pour the puree into a 1-gallon resealable plastic freezer bag and allow the mixture to rest for 10 minutes. Add the meat strips to the marinade and mix them around so they get completely coated with the marinade. Remove as much air as possible from the bag, seal, and place it in the refrigerator for 8 to 24 hours. During the marinating time, remove the bag from the refrigerator and work the meat around so the marinade is fully incorporated in it. Remove the strips from the marinade and arrange in a single layer in your choice of dryer. Dry as directed on pages 16–19.

Venison Jerky

The hunter's saving grace. What do hunters make after they bag their first deer? Jerky. That's what they eat on their next outing. While venison (in this case, deer) can sometimes be gamey tasting, using the lean loin meat to make this jerky helps tremendously in cutting down on the gaminess factor. I'm not a fan of venison meat, but I couldn't stop eating this rich and garlicky jerky and my deer-hunting friends are looking forward to next season's bounty. So am I.

INGREDIENTS

½ cup soy sauce

¼ cup red wine vinegar

4 garlic cloves, crushed

2 teaspoons ground black pepper

½ teaspoon cayenne pepper

1 pound venison strips

INSTRUCTIONS

1. In a 1-gallon resealable plastic freezer bag, thoroughly mix together all the ingredients, except the meat, and allow the mixture to rest for 10 minutes. Add the meat strips to the marinade and mix them around so they get completely coated with the marinade. Remove as much air as possible from the bag, seal, and place it in the refrigerator for 8 to 24 hours. During the marinating time, remove the bag from the refrigerator and work the meat around so the marinade is fully incorporated into it. Remove the strips from the marinade and arrange in a single layer in your choice of dryer. Dry as directed on pages 16–19.

Snappin' Alligator Jerky

Do you hear that? It's the Bayou calling and it's telling you it's time to expand your horizons and try some alligator. While they say it tastes like chicken, it doesn't really. It does have the consistency of chicken, though, with a mild flavor. When you turn it into jerky, it becomes a snack you just can't stop eating.

INGREDIENTS

½ cup soy sauce

¼ cup brown sugar

1 tablespoon pure grade B maple syrup

1 tablespoon sugar

2 teaspoons kosher salt

1 teaspoon red pepper flakes

1 teaspoon liquid hickory smoke

½ teaspoon granulated garlic

½ teaspoon ground black pepper

1 pound alligator loin strips

INSTRUCTIONS

1. In a 1-gallon resealable plastic freezer bag, thoroughly mix together all the ingredients, except the meat, and allow the mixture to rest for 10 minutes. Add the meat strips to the marinade and mix them around so they get completely coated with the marinade. Remove as much air as possible from the bag, seal, and place it in the refrigerator for 8 to 24 hours. During the marinating time, remove the bag from the refrigerator and work the meat around so the marinade is fully incorporated into it. Remove the strips from the marinade and arrange in a single layer in your choice of dryer. Dry as directed on pages 16–19.

Duck à l'Orange Jerky

If you like duck à l'orange but not the fancy restaurants you have to go to, to get it, then this jerky is for you. I like to think of this as fancy-schmancy goes redneck. It's got just the right amount of orange flavor to enhance, but not overwhelm, the duck, and a great herbal flavor from the thyme.

INGREDIENTS

¼ cup frozen orange juice concentrate

¼ cup soy sauce

2 tablespoons sugar

2 tablespoons red wine vinegar

2 teaspoons kosher salt

½ teaspoon ground black pepper

½ teaspoon dried thyme

1 pound boneless, skinless duck breast strips

INSTRUCTIONS

1. In a 1-gallon resealable plastic freezer bag, thoroughly mix together all the ingredients, except the duck, and allow the mixture to rest for 10 minutes. Add the meat strips to the marinade and mix them around so they get completely coated with the marinade. Remove as much air as possible from the bag, seal, and place it in the refrigerator for 8 to 24 hours. During the marinating time, remove the bag from the refrigerator and work the duck around so the marinade is fully incorporated into it. Remove the strips from the marinade and arrange in a single layer in your choice of dryer. Dry as directed on pages 16–19.

Duck Jerky

If you love the rich flavor of duck meat and duck fat, this is a jerky you must make now! The marinade used in this jerky only enhances that rich duck flavor; it doesn't compete with it. For, as fatty as duck can be, it's all in the skin, so once that's removed, the duck meat tends to dry even a bit faster than lean turkey breast does.

INGREDIENTS

⅔ cup soy sauce

⅓ cup Worcestershire sauce

3 tablespoons brown sugar

1 teaspoon granulated garlic

1 teaspoon ground black pepper

¼ teaspoon cayenne pepper

3 to 4 sprigs fresh thyme

1 pound boneless, skinless duck breast strips

INSTRUCTIONS

1. In a 1-gallon resealable plastic freezer bag, thoroughly mix together all the ingredients, except the duck, and allow the mixture to rest for 10 minutes. Add the duck strips to the marinade and mix them around so they get completely coated with the marinade. Remove as much air as possible from the bag, seal, and place it in the refrigerator for 8 to 24 hours. During the marinating time, remove the bag from the refrigerator and work the duck around so the marinade is fully incorporated into it. Remove the strips from the marinade and arrange in a single layer in your choice of dryer. Dry as directed on pages 16–19.

Yakity Yak Jerky

Yak isn't something you come by at your local convenience store, but it's definitely worth the time and effort to find some of this delicious meat. It's ridiculously low in fat and has more protein than beef and more omega-3s than fish. The deep red color of the meat will tell you how rich tasting it is. This jerky is out-of-this-world delicious. I might have to make a trip to Tibet.

INGREDIENTS

- 1 teaspoon granulated garlic
- ½ cup soy sauce
- ¼ cup Worcestershire sauce
- ¼ cup brown sugar
- 1 teaspoon liquid hickory smoke
- 1 teaspoon granulated onion
- 1 tablespoon orange juice concentrate
- 2 teaspoons red wine vinegar
- ½ teaspoon ground black pepper
- 2 pounds yak, cut into slabs

INSTRUCTIONS

1. In a 1-gallon resealable plastic freezer bag, thoroughly mix together all the ingredients, except the meat, and allow the mixture to rest for 10 minutes. Add the meat to the marinade and mix the slabs around so they get completely coated with the marinade. Remove as much air as possible from the bag, seal, and place it in the refrigerator for 8 to 24 hours. During the marinating time, remove the bag from the refrigerator and work the meat around so the marinade is fully incorporated into it. Remove slabs from marinade and arrange in a single layer in your choice of dryer. Dry as directed on pages 16–19.

Game 158 Jerky Everything

Hog Wild Boar Jerky

While wild boar is similar in flavor to its domestic cousin, the pig, the meat itself has a slightly sweeter flavor. This recipe adds a little more sweetness to the party and adds some smoky goodness along with a couple of different pepper flavors. I cut this one into slabs and everyone really enjoyed the chewiness and flavors.

INGREDIENTS

½ cup soy sauce

½ cup pineapple juice

¼ cup teriyaki sauce

2 tablespoons brown sugar

1½ teaspoons liquid hickory smoke

1½ teaspoons granulated garlic

1 teaspoon ground black pepper

½ teaspoon ground white pepper

1 pound wild boar loin, cut into slabs

INSTRUCTIONS

1. In a 1-gallon resealable plastic freezer bag, thoroughly mix together all the ingredients, except the meat, and allow the mixture to rest for 10 minutes. Add the meat slabs to the marinade and mix them around so they get completely coated with the marinade. Remove as much air as possible from the bag, seal, and place it in the refrigerator for 8 to 24 hours. During the marinating time, remove the bag from the refrigerator and work the meat around so the marinade is fully incorporated into it. Remove the slabs from the marinade and arrange in a single layer in your choice of dryer. Dry as directed on pages 16–19.

CHAPTER 5

Poltry

A type of jerky that seems to be gaining in popularity right now is turkey jerky, and why not? Turkey is lighter and lower in calories than beef and it's good for you, too. One of the things that I like about using turkey is that it's got a light flavor; that means I can make up some pretty bold-flavored marinades.

I found that I was greatly influenced by the potato chip aisle when I was working on the turkey marinades, so some of these flavor combinations might sound familiar to you. But turkey jerky is *a lot* better for you than scarfing down a bag of potato chips . . . even when those chips are baked.

A few tips to make your turkey jerky-making life easier:

- Wear gloves when you're working with raw poultry. Poultry has its own bacterial issues, so wearing the gloves will help cut down on cross-contamination. It's also important that everything you use on poultry is very clean. You can't be too clean when it comes to working with poultry.

- Buying the boneless, skinless turkey tenderloins will save you the most headaches. There's no need for boning, skinning, or even prefreezing. Because these are so thick, you can cut them to ⅛- to ¼-inch-thick slices pretty easily without having to freeze them. But you certainly can partially freeze them first, if you like. (No defrosting already frozen turkey in the microwave, though.)

- When working with turkey breasts, always freeze them for 30 to 40 minutes before attempting to slice them.

- If you do buy bone-in, skin-on turkey breasts, you will definitely need to prefreeze them for about 40 minutes after de-boning them and before slicing them.

- Like other meats, turkey can be cut into slabs or strips, but even if you cut it into slabs it won't be as tough as beef slabs. Turkey is just a more tender meat. I prefer to cut turkey into slabs.

Garlic Dill Turkey

Do you like a dill pickle with your turkey deli sandwich? Skip all the extras because this turkey jerky has the pucker power of dill pickles with a good bit of garlic pow for added flavor. Hey, it worked for potato chips . . . it can work for jerky.

INGREDIENTS

Juice from a 24-ounce jar of dill pickles

4 garlic cloves, crushed

1 pound turkey breast slabs

INSTRUCTIONS

1. In a 1-gallon resealable plastic freezer bag, thoroughly mix together all the ingredients, except the turkey, and allow the mixture to rest for 10 minutes. Add the turkey strips to the marinade and mix them around so they get completely coated with the marinade. Remove as much air as possible from the bag, seal, and place it in the refrigerator for 8 to 24 hours. During the marinating time, remove the bag from the refrigerator and work the turkey around so the marinade is fully incorporated into it. Remove the strips from the marinade and arrange in a single layer in your choice of dryer. Dry as directed on pages 16–19.

Thanksgiving Day Jerky

That fourth Thursday in November is a magical day, isn't it? Well, excluding the family part and the travel part. A day of food, football, and more food—what a combo; and let's not forget about the star of the show . . . the turkey. Don't you wish you could have that delicious Thanksgiving turkey without all the people and dishes? This turkey jerky will have you savoring Thanksgiving dinner all over again, minus the cranberries and the annoying questions from your family.

INGREDIENTS

¼ cup salt

2 tablespoons brown sugar

2 tablespoons poultry seasoning

Generous ¼ teaspoon freshly ground pepper

2 pounds turkey breast slabs

INSTRUCTIONS

1. In a small bowl, thoroughly mix all the ingredients together, except the turkey, and allow the mixture to rest for 10 minutes. Place the turkey strips in a 1-gallon resealable plastic freezer bag and add the dry rub. Mix the slabs around so they are completely coated with the dry rub. Remove as much air as possible from the bag, seal, and place it in the refrigerator for 8 to 24 hours. During the marinating time, remove the bag from the refrigerator and work the turkey around so the rub is fully incorporated into it. Remove the slabs from the rub and arrange in a single layer in your choice of dryer. Dry as directed on pages 16–19.

Sea Salt and Vinegar Jerky

No, I'm not talking about the potato chips here, but aren't those the best? After devouring a bag of those salty delights, I thought I'd turn the sea salt and vinegar treatment on to some turkey jerky. This combo tastes even better than the chips. You'll swear you're eating potato chips while you munch down on this *much* healthier snack. There's not a lot of protein in those potato chips, but there is in the turkey. Dig into this tangy treat!

INGREDIENTS

1½ tablespoons brown sugar

1½ tablespoons fine sea salt

A few grinds of black pepper

¾ cup cider vinegar

1½ to 2 pounds turkey breast slabs

INSTRUCTIONS

1. In a bowl, thoroughly mix together all the ingredients, except the vinegar and turkey. Pour the vinegar into a wide bowl. Dip the turkey into the vinegar and place in a 1-gallon resealable plastic freezer bag. Add the dry rub and mix the strips around so they get completely coated with the rub. Remove as much air as possible from the bag, seal, and place it in the refrigerator for 8 to 24 hours. During the marinating time, remove the bag from the refrigerator and work the turkey around so the rub is fully incorporated into it. Remove the strips from the rub and arrange in a single layer in your choice of dryer. Dry as directed on pages 16–19.

Buffalo Belle Jerky

Yes, **this really does taste like the famous wings (minus the pesky bones and all that grease).** I used a hybrid recipe for the classic Buffalo wings and marinated turkey breast meat with it. Then, just before dehydrating, I topped it with dehydrated blue cheese. Even though the cheese is dried, it still offsets the heat from the red hot sauce, just like the regular hot wings. All you need now is celery sticks and an ice-cold beer.

INGREDIENTS

6 tablespoons Frank's red hot sauce

1½ tablespoons white vinegar

1 teaspoon sugar

1 teaspoon salt

¼ teaspoon cayenne pepper

¼ teaspoon Worcestershire sauce

¼ teaspoon smoked paprika

¼ teaspoon granulated garlic

⅛ teaspoon ground black pepper

1 pound turkey breast meat slabs

Dehydrated blue cheese crumbles (see page 198) or powdered blue cheese

INSTRUCTIONS

1. In a 1-gallon resealable plastic freezer bag, thoroughly mix together all the ingredients, except the turkey and cheese, and allow the mixture to rest for 10 minutes. Add the turkey strips to the marinade and mix them around so they get completely coated with the marinade. Remove as much air as possible from the bag, seal, and place it in the refrigerator for 8 to 24 hours. During the marinating time, remove the bag from the refrigerator and work the turkey around so the marinade is fully incorporated into it. Remove the strips from the marinade and arrange in a single layer in your choice of dryer. Sprinkle the cheese crumbles or powdered cheese liberally over the marinated turkey before starting the drying process. Dry as directed on pages 16–19.

Lemon Garlic Turkey

Lemon pepper might be the old standby seasoning, but after you take one bite of this turkey jerky, you're going to be hooked on lemon garlic! Really! The flavors in this are really strong, and that's a good thing. I'm pretty sure after having your first batch of this lemon garlic turkey jerky, you're going to go cold turkey (get it?) on potato chips. Just remember to share, cuz no one likes a jerky hog. So make a big batch of this, because you're probably not going to want to share.

INGREDIENTS

½ cup soy sauce

¼ cup + 2 tablespoons lemon juice

2 tablespoons agave nectar

1 tablespoon granulated garlic

1 teaspoon ground black pepper

Zest of 1 lemon

1 pound turkey breast slabs

INSTRUCTIONS

1. In a 1-gallon resealable plastic freezer bag, thoroughly mix together all the ingredients, except the turkey, and allow the mixture to rest for 10 minutes. Add the turkey strips to the marinade and mix them around so they get completely coated with the marinade. Remove as much air as possible from the bag, seal, and place it in the refrigerator for 4 to 6 hours. During the marinating time, remove the bag from the refrigerator and work the turkey around so the marinade is fully incorporated into it. Remove the strips from the marinade and arrange in a single layer in your choice of dryer. Dry as directed on pages 16–19.

Sweet & Spicy Turkey Jerky

Turkey is a great base for jerky because it doesn't have a strong flavor. That means whatever you put on it, you can really taste. This sweet and spicy jerky has the perfect balance of both, so you're not overwhelmed by sweetness or heat. And who wants to have to make a choice between sweet or heat?

INGREDIENTS

½ cup soy sauce

½ cup sweet chili sauce

1 teaspoon brown sugar

1 teaspoon red pepper flakes

1 pound turkey breast slabs

INSTRUCTIONS

1. In a 1-gallon resealable plastic freezer bag, thoroughly mix together all the ingredients, except the turkey, and allow the mixture to rest for 10 minutes. Add the turkey strips to the marinade and mix them around so they get completely coated with the marinade. Remove as much air as possible from the bag, seal, and place it in the refrigerator for 8 to 24 hours. During the marinating time, remove the bag from the refrigerator and work the turkey around so the marinade is fully incorporated into it. Remove the strips from the marinade and arrange in a single layer in your choice of dryer. Dry as directed on pages 16–19.

Honey Jalapeño Ranch Jerky

Let me start by saying that this is not a hot and spicy jerky. You'll actually taste the flavor of the jalapeño. Yes, hot peppers do have a flavor beyond the fire. This is one of my favorite jerkies. I'm a big fan of ranch dressing; isn't everyone? The addition of honey and the pepper give the ranch a more grown-up and slightly sophisticated flavor.

INGREDIENTS

¼ cup water

¼ cup ranch dressing seasoning mix

3 tablespoons honey

2 tablespoons cider vinegar

2 tablespoons soy sauce

1 jalapeño pepper, stemmed and roughly chopped

½ teaspoon salt

1½ pounds turkey breast slabs

INSTRUCTIONS

1. Toss all the ingredients, except the turkey, into a food processor and buzz until everything is pureed. Pour the puree into a 1-gallon resealable plastic freezer bag and allow the mixture to rest for 10 minutes. Add the turkey strips to the marinade and mix them around so they get completely coated with the marinade. Remove as much air as possible from the bag, seal, and place it in the refrigerator for 8 to 24 hours. During the marinating time, remove the bag from the refrigerator and work the turkey around so the marinade is fully incorporated into it. Remove the strips from the marinade and arrange in a single layer in your choice of dryer. Dry as directed on pages 16–19.

Cheddar Jalapeño Turkey Jerky

This is another flavor that was inspired by a bag of potato chips.
I might have a serious potato chip problem. The tangy Cheddar cheese and zippy flavor of the jalapeños definitely perk up the flavor of the turkey. Yes, you can still taste the turkey through both of these strong flavors. But putting the bag of this jerky down is gonna be tough.

INGREDIENTS

½ cup cider vinegar

1 jalapeño pepper, roughly chopped

3 tablespoons Cheddar cheese powder

1 tablespoon powdered buttermilk

1 tablespoon lemon juice

1 teaspoon salt

½ teaspoon onion powder

1 pound turkey breast slabs

INSTRUCTIONS

1. Toss all the ingredients, except the turkey, into a food processor and buzz until everything is pureed. Pour the puree into a 1-gallon resealable plastic freezer bag and allow the mixture to rest for 10 minutes. Add the turkey strips to the marinade and mix them around so they get completely coated with the marinade. Remove as much air as possible from the bag, seal, and place it in the refrigerator for 8 to 24 hours. During the marinating time, remove the bag from the refrigerator and work the turkey around so the marinade is fully incorporated into it. Remove the strips from the marinade and arrange in a single layer in your choice of dryer. Dry as directed on pages 16–19.

Orange Ginger Turkey Jerky

This one is what it says! There's a lot of orange flavor when you first start into this jerky. As you continue chewing, you'll start to get that familiar ginger tingle on your tongue and taste its lemon peppery flavor. Even though these flavors are strong, you can still taste the turkey, and what a great combo of flavors these are for turkey.

INGREDIENTS

¼ cup frozen orange juice concentrate

¼ cup soy sauce

2 tablespoons granulated ginger

2 tablespoons water

2 tablespoons kosher salt

1 tablespoon orange zest

1 tablespoon brown sugar

2 teaspoons granulated onion

1 teaspoon granulated garlic

1 teaspoon red pepper flakes

1 pound turkey breast slabs

INSTRUCTIONS

1. In a 1-gallon resealable plastic freezer bag, thoroughly mix together all the ingredients, except the turkey, and allow the mixture to rest for 10 minutes. Add the turkey strips to the marinade and mix them around so they get completely coated with the marinade. Remove as much air as possible from the bag, seal, and place it in the refrigerator for 8 to 24 hours. During the marinating time, remove the bag from the refrigerator and work the turkey around so the marinade is fully incorporated into it. Remove the strips from the marinade and arrange in a single layer in your choice of dryer. Dry as directed on pages 16–19.

Chipotle Cheddar Turkey Jerky

Yes, it's another Cheddar-pepper combo, but this one has the added benefit of a rich, smoky flavor.

It's interesting how these flavors work so well with pork, beef, or poultry. I just couldn't resist unleashing this flavor on boring ol' turkey. It's kind of like screaming, *"Wake up, turkey!"* but in a much subtler way, so you don't wake the entire neighborhood.

INGREDIENTS

½ cup cider vinegar

1 chipotle pepper + 1 teaspoon adobo sauce (from canned chipotles in adobo)

3 tablespoons Cheddar cheese powder

1 tablespoon powdered buttermilk

1 tablespoon lemon juice

1 teaspoon salt

½ teaspoon onion powder

1 pound turkey breast slabs

INSTRUCTIONS

1. Toss all the ingredients, except the turkey, into a food processor and buzz until everything is pureed. Pour the puree into a 1-gallon resealable plastic freezer bag and allow the mixture to rest for 10 minutes. Add the turkey strips to the marinade and mix them around so they get completely coated with the marinade. Remove as much air as possible from the bag, seal, and place it in the refrigerator for 8 to 24 hours. During the marinating time, remove the bag from the refrigerator and work the turkey around so the marinade is fully incorporated into it. Remove the strips from the marinade and arrange in a single layer in your choice of dryer. Dry as directed on pages 16–19.

Quick Nacho Cheese Turkey Jerky

Bust open your microwave door for this quick and easy jerky and you can be eating the deliciousness in less than ten minutes (start to finish). Not only is this jerky fast to make, but it's a Paleo godsend for when you get the munchies and just know eating that bag of tortilla chips is going to do you in. This jerky is a little chewy, but mostly on the crunchy side.

INGREDIENTS

2 teaspoons taco seasoning mix

2 teaspoons Cheddar cheese powder

1 pound deli sliced turkey, cut into strips

INSTRUCTIONS

1. In a medium-size bowl, mix together all the ingredients, except the turkey. Line a microwave bacon cooker or microwave-safe dish with a layer of paper towels. Arrange the turkey strips in a single layer on the paper towels and sprinkle with the cheese powder. Cover the meat with another paper towel and put into the microwave. Cook for 1½ minutes on high, then flip the meat over, re-cover, and cook for another 1½ minutes on high. Repeat this step one more time. If it's done to your liking, let it cool, then eat. Otherwise, repeat the cooking steps in 30-second intervals until the desired doneness is reached. The turkey will get pretty brown in spots, but that's okay . . . it's just getting good and crisp.

CHAPTER 6

Fish

There have been plenty of arguments regarding fish jerky while I've been writing this book. Things like "Can you call dried fish jerky?" Or just a very emphatic "Fish isn't jerky." Or then, there's "Fish jerky tastes terrible . . . who eats that stuff?"

Well, fish jerky is very real, you can call it jerky and it doesn't taste terrible if you use the right kind of fish and flavorings. Fish jerky has become very popular on a retail level because it is so high in protein and has lots of healthy benefits not found in beef or poultry.

A few tips to make your jerky making life easier:

- Wear those gloves. Keeping your work area clean is especially important when working with fish.

- Always choose wild fish over farmed fish. It's better for the environment and wild fish tastes so much better.

- Lower-fat fish is best to work with. Cod and tuna are popular choices. Having said that, salmon is a fantastic fish to make into jerky. Removing the skin is also a good idea to reduce the fat, unless you like to eat the skin. Then make sure to remove as much oil as you can with the paper towels (as discussed earlier).

- For tuna, you'll most likely be buying steaks, but for all other fish, use fillets. A fillet lets you get a much thinner piece of fish cut for the jerky.

- Go easy on the salt, if you're making your own marinade. Fish is pretty light tasting and has a tendency to really absorb salt.

- While citrus tastes wonderful on fish, if you choose to make a marinade containing citrus, you won't be able to let the fish marinate for very long. Citrus juice "cooks" fish proteins and

you will end up with a very odd-textured piece of jerky. So just avoid citrus marinades on fish. If you really like lemon on your fish, squeeze a lemon over the fish just before dehydrating it. You'll get the flavor and the fish won't "cook" in the juice.

- Season your fish the same way you would if you were cooking it. Spicy sauces and sweet teriyaki taste great on both tuna and salmon.

- It's okay to use frozen fish to make jerky, too. Do not thaw the fish in the microwave, though. A lot of times the fish actually ends up cooking in the microwave and that will change the consistency and flavor of your jerky. Thaw it in the refrigerator.

- Cut the fish into ¼-inch-thick slices or slabs. This way, they will dry evenly.

- If you use a very sweet sauce on the salmon, you may find that your salmon is almost candied once it has dried. Don't panic; it's fine—it will just look translucent and not opaque as dried fish usually does. It will taste fantastic!

Ginger Wasabi Jerky

If you eat sushi, you're more than familiar with what this tastes like. But in jerky form, it takes on a whole other level of flavors. Because so much of the moisture is removed, all of the flavors are concentrated. This also uses wasabi powder, which has a different flavor (not as pungent) when it's mixed with a lot more liquid than usual. This one tastes like an old friend, for all you sushi lovers out there.

INGREDIENTS

¾ cup soy sauce

½ cup mirin

2 dried Thai bird chiles, crushed

3 tablespoons wasabi powder

2 tablespoons brown sugar

2 tablespoons lime juice

1 tablespoon peeled and grated fresh ginger

½ teaspoon ground black pepper

1 pound ahi tuna strips

INSTRUCTIONS

1. In a 1-gallon resealable plastic freezer bag, thoroughly mix together all the ingredients, except the fish, and allow the mixture to rest for 10 minutes. Add the fish strips to the marinade and mix them around so they get completely coated with the marinade. Remove as much air as possible from the bag, seal, and place it in the refrigerator for 8 to 24 hours. During the marinating time, remove the bag from the refrigerator and work the fish around so the marinade is fully incorporated into it. Remove the strips from the marinade and arrange in a single layer in your choice of dryer. Dry as directed on pages 16–19.

Teriyaki Tuna Jerky

I know, I know, fish jerky is kinda weird, but it's very good for you because it's so lean. This jerky is a bit surprising in that you can taste that it is made from tuna, but the teriyaki flavor is just a bit stronger.

INGREDIENTS

2 cups pineapple juice

1 teaspoon powdered ginger

1 teaspoon fine sea salt

½ teaspoon granulated garlic

⅛ teaspoon onion powder

⅛ teaspoon ground nutmeg

⅛ teaspoon ground black pepper

6 drops liquid hickory smoke

1 to 1 ½ pounds ahi tuna strips

INSTRUCTIONS

1. In a 1-gallon resealable plastic freezer bag, thoroughly mix together all the ingredients, except the fish, and allow the mixture to rest for 10 minutes. Add the fish strips to the marinade and mix them around so they get completely coated with the marinade. Remove as much air as possible from the bag, seal, and place it in the refrigerator for 8 to 24 hours. During the marinating time, remove the bag from the refrigerator and work the fish around so the marinade is fully incorporated into it. Remove the strips from the marinade and arrange in a single layer in your choice of dryer. Dry as directed on pages 16–19.

Ginger Chile Salmon Jerky

You're probably familiar with smoked salmon or the cured salmon also known as lox. Well, if you like those, you're going to love salmon jerky. With all the health benefits of salmon, such as omega-3s, amino acids, and more protein than the same size serving of beef, the fact that it tastes amazing is just an added benefit. The tangy citrusy flavor of ginger combined with the zing of chili oil gives the rich taste of salmon and a kick.

INGREDIENTS

2 tablespoons brown sugar

1 tablespoon peeled and grated fresh ginger

1 tablespoon chili oil (with seeds)

1 tablespoon unseasoned rice vinegar

2 teaspoons kosher salt

1 pound wild salmon strips (skin removed)

INSTRUCTIONS

1. In a 1-gallon resealable plastic freezer bag, thoroughly mix together all the ingredients, except the fish, and allow the mixture to rest for 10 minutes. Add the fish strips to the marinade and mix them around so they get completely coated with the marinade. Remove as much air as possible from the bag, seal, and place it in the refrigerator for 8 to 24 hours. During the marinating time, remove the bag from the refrigerator and work the fish around so the marinade is fully incorporated into it. Remove the strips from the marinade and arrange in a single layer in your choice of dryer. Dry as directed on pages 16–19.

Miso Salmon Jerky

This is a takeoff on the popular ginger miso eggplant dish that's on so many restaurant menus. The salty miso paired with sweet mirin is a classic combination for the rich taste of salmon and makes a perfect match. All the benefits of adding salmon to your diet are just a healthy bonus to great flavor.

INGREDIENTS

¼ cup shiro (white miso)

¼ cup mirin

¼ cup soy sauce

2 tablespoons unseasoned rice vinegar

2 teaspoons ground ginger

1 tablespoon sugar

1 teaspoon sesame oil

1 teaspoon onion powder

1 pound wild salmon strips (skin removed)

INSTRUCTIONS

1. In a 1-gallon resealable plastic freezer bag, thoroughly mix together all the ingredients, except the fish, and allow the mixture to rest for 10 minutes. Add the fish strips to the marinade and mix them around so they get completely coated with the marinade. Remove as much air as possible from the bag, seal, and place it in the refrigerator for 8 to 24 hours. During the marinating time, remove the bag from the refrigerator and work the fish around so the marinade is fully incorporated into it. Remove the strips from the marinade and arrange in a single layer in your choice of dryer. Dry as directed on pages 16–19.

Salted Lemon Mahi Mahi Jerky

Mahi Mahi is a light tasting fish that lends itself well to jerky making. Sure there's a slight bit of fish flavor, but not as much tuna or salmon. If you prefer, you could use snapper in this recipe instead.

INGREDIENTS

¼ cup soy sauce

¼ cup mirin

2 tablespoons sugar

1 teaspoon sesame oil

1 teaspoon ginger powder

1 teaspoon freshly ground black pepper

1 teaspoon citric acid

½ teaspoon granulated onion

½ teaspoon granulated garlic

Zest of 1 whole lemon

Juice from half of 1 lemon

1 pound wild mahi mahi strips

INSTRUCTIONS

1. In a 1-gallon resealable plastic freezer bag, thoroughly mix together all the ingredients, except the fish, and allow the mixture to rest for 10 minutes. Add the fish strips to the marinade and mix them around so that they get completely coated with the marinade. Remove as much air as possible from the bag, seal, and place it in the refrigerator for 4 hours. During the marinating time, remove the bag from the refrigerator and work the fish around so that the marinade is fully incorporated into it. Remove strips from marinade and arrange in a single layer in your choice of dryer. Dry as directed on pages 16–19.

CHAPTER 7

Vegetarian

Why is there a vegetarian section in a jerky book, you ask. Because it's my book and I like to push the boundaries a little bit. Plus, a lot of people out there have decided not to eat meat anymore and I thought they, too, would like some of these delicious, chewy snacks.

I will warn you, a lot of these vegetarian recipes are quite addicting. Addicting to the point that you'll forget that you're not eating meat . . . or you just won't care.

These recipes aren't all just tofu (okay, a couple are), but I used mushrooms, vegetables, and different fruits for some great little dessert jerkies for your eating pleasure. Heck, there's even a cocktail-inspired jerky in this section.

This is the one section of recipes where my statement "You can use these marinades on anything in the book" probably won't hold up. Once you get into the recipes, you'll see why.

But don't just turn your nose up at this section just because you're a carnivore at heart and wouldn't think of eating a jerky that's made from anything but meat. I had a bunch of big, burly hockey guys eating one of the tofu jerkies and loving it so much, they ate every last crumb and asked for more.

Tofu Cheddar Crazy Jerky

Even vegetarians like jerky. Maybe not the traditional meat jerky, but tofu makes a fantastic base for jerky. This vegan jerky gets its rich cheesy flavor from nutritional yeast and a spicy little kick from a pinch of cayenne pepper. I fed this to a bunch of meat-eating hockey players (none of whom knew what tofu even was) and they inhaled it and asked for more. So take that you tofu scoffers!

INGREDIENTS

2 tablespoons lemon juice

2 tablespoons nutritional yeast

1 teaspoon sea salt

Pinch of cayenne pepper (optional)

1 (12-ounce) package extra-firm tofu, drained and sliced into 24 strips

INSTRUCTIONS

1. In a small bowl, thoroughly mix together all the ingredients, except the tofu, and allow the mixture to rest for 10 minutes. Liberally brush the tofu strips, on all sides, with the lemon juice mixture and arrange on drying racks in a single layer. Dry at 115°F as directed on pages 16–19 for 4 to 6 hours.

Portobello Bacon Jerky

This is another vegan jerky that nonvegans are gonna love. I realize there's "bacon" in the name, but it only tastes as if there's bacon in it. Trust me on this. They already grill giant portobello mushroom caps and make "burgers" out of them at restaurants, so why not jerky? Drying the portobellos gives you the same chewy consistency as sliced beef, too. So it really does have your mouth and brain thinking jerky and not just mushroom. Plus, *bacon*! What else do I need to say? Just try it, you big meat eater; you're really going to like it.

INGREDIENTS

3 tablespoons liquid aminos

2 tablespoons pure maple syrup (grade B)

2 tablespoons cider vinegar

1 teaspoon paprika

½ teaspoon smoked paprika

¼ teaspoon smoked salt

A few grinds of black pepper

1 (8-ounce) package portobello mushrooms, sliced ¼-inch thick

INSTRUCTIONS

1. In a 1-gallon resealable plastic freezer bag, thoroughly mix together all the ingredients, except the mushrooms, and allow the mixture to rest for 10 minutes. Add the mushroom slices to the marinade and mix them around so they get completely coated with the marinade. Remove as much air as possible from the bag, seal, and place it in the refrigerator for 4 hours. During the marinating time, remove the bag from the refrigerator and carefully work the mushroom slices around so the marinade is fully incorporated into them. Remove the slices from marinade and arrange in a single layer in your choice of dryer. Dry at 145°F as directed on pages 16–19 for 4 to 6 hours.

Mellow Mushroom Jerky

This vegan jerky is very similar to the Portobello Bacon Jerky, but the flavors aren't as strong. It still has all the umami that cooked mushrooms have, but the seasonings are mellower. Eating this jerky is like listening to a Coldplay song, but in a good way.

INGREDIENTS

- 3 tablespoons liquid aminos
- 2 tablespoons pure maple syrup (grade B)
- 2 tablespoons cider vinegar
- 1 teaspoon Chinese five-spice powder
- ¼ teaspoon smoked salt
- A few grinds of black pepper
- 1 (8-ounce) package portobello mushrooms, sliced ¼-inch thick

INSTRUCTIONS

1. In a 1-gallon resealable plastic freezer bag, thoroughly mix together all the ingredients, except the mushrooms, and allow the mixture to rest for 10 minutes. Add the mushroom slices to the marinade and mix them around so they get completely coated with the marinade. Remove as much air as possible from the bag, seal, and place it in the refrigerator for 8 to 24 hours. During the marinating time, remove the bag from the refrigerator and work the slices around so the marinade is fully incorporated into them. Remove the strips from the marinade and arrange in a single layer in your choice of dryer. Dry at 145°F as directed on pages 16–19 for 4 to 6 hours.

Ginger Miso Eggplant Jerky (a.k.a. Nasu Dengaku)

Japanese ginger miso eggplant makes frequent appearances on restaurant menus probably because it's a little bit sweet, a little bit salty, and has lots of that mysterious umami flavor you hear so much about. It's also a really easy dish to make. But while it tastes delicious, it's got a pretty slimy texture which turns a lot of people off, including me. Mushy eggplant is just kinda gross—right? The slightly crisp, and definitely chewy, texture of the jerky version of this dish tastes even better than its restaurant version because it's not slimy.

INGREDIENTS

- 6 tablespoons shiro (white miso)
- 3 tablespoons unseasoned rice vinegar
- 1½ tablespoons water
- 1 tablespoon grated fresh ginger
- 2 teaspoons sesame oil
- 1 teaspoon soy sauce (or use tamari to make this vegan-friendly and gluten free)
- 2 medium-size eggplants (roughly 2 pounds), cut into ¼-inch circles

INSTRUCTIONS

1. In a 1-gallon resealable plastic freezer bag, thoroughly mix together all the ingredients, except the eggplant, and allow the mixture to rest for 10 minutes. Add the eggplant to the paste and mix them around so they get completely coated with the marinade. Remove as much air as possible from the bag, seal, and place it in the refrigerator for 8 to 24 hours. During the marinating time, remove the bag from the refrigerator and work the eggplant around so the paste is fully incorporated into it. Remove the eggplant from the paste and arrange in a single layer in your choice of dryer. Dry at 145°F as directed on pages 16–19 for 4 to 6 hours.

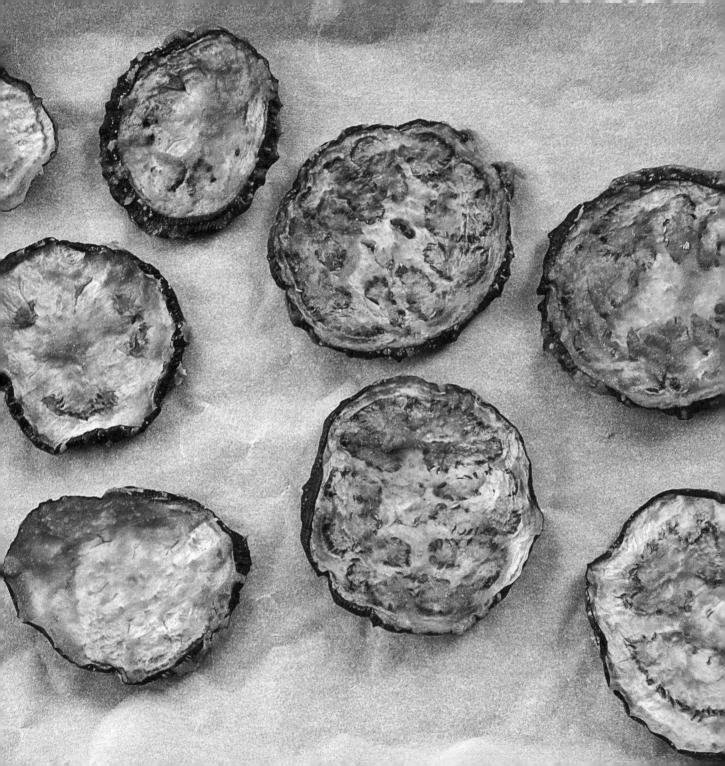

Chile Lime Mango Jerky

You've definitely seen packages of dried chile mangoes at the store, but did you know you could dehydrate the fruit at home and it tastes waaaaaaayyyyy better?

Because there are no preservatives in the homemade version, it stays that bright, pretty, yellow-orange color. Adding the touch of tart lime juice to the sweet mango gives it another great layer of flavor that goes great with the heat of the cayenne.

INGREDIENTS

¼ cup lime juice

2 ripe mangoes, peeled, pitted, and cut into ¼-inch slices

Cayenne pepper

Kosher salt

INSTRUCTIONS

1. Pour the lime juice into a wide bowl. Dip the mango slices into the lime juice and arrange in a single layer on a drying rack. Sprinkle lightly with cayenne and salt to taste. Proceed to dry at 145°F as directed on pages 16–19 for 3 to 4 hours.

Dehydrated Blue Cheese

Yes, this takes forever to make and, yes, it's worth it, so you want to do it. Your alternative is to buy blue cheese powder. The powder works, but it definitely doesn't look as pretty on the finished product.

8 ounce piece of Maytag blue cheese
(or crumbly blue cheese of your choice)

INSTRUCTIONS

1. Lay the fruit roll dryer sheet on top of the drying rack (so the cheese doesn't fall through). Break up the cheese into small, uniformly sized pieces. Allow space between the cheese pieces so the air can circulate and dry it. Dry for at least 12 hours at 115°F as directed on pages 16–19. Around hour 4, and again around hour 6, break up any of the larger pieces so they will dry. Store in an airtight container.

Blueberry Fruit Leather

Technically this isn't jerky, but it can be made in the dehydrator or oven and it is very chewy stuff, so I thought I'd include it. I love that I can make my own fruit leather and really know what's actually in it. Plus, those puny little rolls of it you buy at the store aren't nearly long enough to satisfy a craving. Now I can make rolls as long as my sheet pan. Oh, and did I mention you can use fresh *or* frozen fruit to make this?

INGREDIENTS

1 cup fresh or frozen blueberries (thawed if frozen)
½ teaspoon lemon juice
¼ teaspoon ground cinnamon
Pinch of kosher salt

INSTRUCTIONS

1. Preheat the oven to 170°F. Line a baking sheet with a silicone sheet or parchment paper. Puree all the ingredients in a blender. Pour and smooth the mixture onto the prepared baking sheet. Place in the preheated oven and place a wooden cooking utensil (or other heat-resistant utensil) handle in the oven door to keep it ajar and allow air to circulate around the fruit leather. Bake for 4½ hours. Start checking it at 3 hours. Fruit leather is done when it feels slightly sticky, but doesn't pull away on your finger. If it cracks when you bend a piece of it, it's been cooked for too long. Let cool, then cut into strips with a very sharp knife or pizza cutter. Leave the strips on the parchment paper, if using, and you can roll them up without the fruit sticking together. Or cut and stack them with waxed paper between each strip.

Simple Coconut Jerky

You already know that coconut water is good for you and tastes best when it comes from a fresh young coconut, not a box. Assuming you can figure out how to get a straw into the coconut. But did you know that the young coconut meat makes an amazing jerky? Well, it does. After you slurp out the electrolyte-laden goodness of the water, you'll want to open that bad boy up (there are videos online that show how to do this). Scoop out the white meat inside the shell and plop it into the marinade. Dehydrate it and chow down on some of the best-tasting coconut/jerky you'll ever eat. Oh yeah, this one's vegan, too. Shhhhh . . .

INGREDIENTS

2 tablespoons tamari

1 tablespoon pure maple syrup (grade B)

⅛ teaspoon ground black pepper

Meat from 2 young coconuts, cut into 2-inch pieces

INSTRUCTIONS

1. In a 1-gallon resealable plastic freezer bag, thoroughly mix together all the ingredients, except the coconut meat, and allow the mixture to rest for 10 minutes. Add the coconut meat to the marinade and mix them around so they get completely coated with the marinade. Remove as much air as possible from the bag, seal, and place it in the refrigerator for 8 to 24 hours. During the marinating time, remove the bag from the refrigerator and work the coconut meat around so the marinade is fully incorporated into it. Remove the coconut meat from the marinade and arrange in a single layer in your choice of dryer. Dry at 135°F as directed on pages 16–19 for 4 to 6 hours.

Chocolate Orange Slices

The combination of chocolate and orange has never been appealing to me. My husband adores it ... so this one's for him. This is a great little tidbit to have on hand for parties. You can leave little dishes of it around the room for people to pick up and nibble on. They most likely won't know what they're eating, but they'll be asking you for the recipe. Even though the outside dries, the inside of the orange still has moisture. When you bite into it, you'll get a burst of orange that mingles with the cocoa and cayenne. This is going to be one of your favorite recipes.

INGREDIENTS

2 large navel oranges

2 tablespoons sugar

1 tablespoon unsweetened cocoa powder

Cayenne pepper

INSTRUCTIONS

1. Slice off the orange skin and make sure to remove the white pith along with the skin. Slice each orange into ¼-inch-thick circles. Layer the slices between paper towels to remove some of the moisture. Pour the sugar into a flat dish. Dip one side of each orange slice into the sugar. Sprinkle that same side with a bit of cocoa and cayenne. Place on mesh dryer sheets in a dehydrator. (If you put them on the regular drying trays, the oranges will stick and rip apart when you try to remove them.) Dry at 135°F as directed on pages 16–19 for 6 to 8 hours.

Tart Cherry Almond Fruit Leather

Same as the blueberry fruit leather, but it's my book so I can put it in here. Almond and cherry is a classic flavor combination (if you crack open a cherry pit, it smells like almonds—try it sometime). I like using tart cherries because I love to eat sour puckery things, but you could use sweet cherries if you prefer the sweeter things in life. Either one will work in this recipe and fresh or frozen fruit is fine.

INGREDIENTS

2 cups fresh or frozen pitted tart or sweet cherries (thawed if frozen)

2 tablespoons sugar, or to taste

1 teaspoon lemon juice

¼ teaspoon almond extract

INSTRUCTIONS

1. Preheat the oven to 170°F. Line a baking sheet with a silicone sheet or parchment paper. Puree all the ingredients in a blender. Pour and smooth the mixture onto the prepared baking sheet. Place in the preheated oven and place a wooden cooking utensil (or other heat-resistant utensil) handle in the oven door to keep it ajar and allow air to circulate around the fruit leather. Bake at 170°F for 4½ hours. Start checking it at 3 hours. Fruit leather is done when it feels slightly sticky, but doesn't pull away on your finger. If it cracks when you bend a piece of it, it's been cooked too long. Let cool then cut into strips with a very sharp knife or pizza cutter. Leave the strips on the parchment paper, if using, and you can roll them up without the fruit sticking together. Or cut and stack them with waxed paper between each strip.

Piña Colada Jerky

Dessert jerky! This is everything you love about the piña colada cocktail in jerky form. There's no meat in this one, just fruit, coconut, and rum . . . . lots of rum. Oh, and there's a lot less fat and calories in this version. Everyone who tries this jerky falls in love with it. I can't stop eating it when I make it. Plus, you can use the leftover rum to make a cocktail or two.

INGREDIENTS

1 whole pineapple

⅔ cup sweetened shredded coconut

1½ cups coconut rum

INSTRUCTIONS

1. Remove the top, bottom, and skin from the pineapple. Slice on a mandoline into ³⁄₁₆-inch rounds. Remove the core from the slices. Layer the pineapple and coconut in an airtight container. Pour the rum over the top. Cover and let sit for 8 to 24 hours, turning over the container several times while marinating to get everything good and soaked. Remove from the marinade and arrange in a single layer in your choice of dryer. (You can save this rum and use it for making tasty cocktails.) Dry at 145°F, following the directions on pages 16–19 for 4 to 6 hours.

Thai Coconut Jerky

Vegan jerky doesn't mean flavorless and this coconut jerky has so much flavor in it, you'll understand after your first bite. I love how coconut meat absorbs the flavors in marinades but still allows you to have a subtle coconut flavor at the same time. This is a really savory jerky, which might surprise you because it's made from coconut and has vanilla in it. The vanilla gives off a warm flavor and the Thai bird chile adds just a touch of heat.

INGREDIENTS

2 stalks lemongrass, sliced into rounds, soft bottom part only

1 cup young coconut water

1 dried Thai bird chile, crushed

2 tablespoons tamari

1½ teaspoons chopped fresh ginger

1 teaspoon vanilla extract

Meat from 2 young coconuts, chopped

INSTRUCTIONS

1. In a 1-gallon resealable plastic freezer bag, thoroughly mix together all the ingredients, except the coconut meat, and allow the mixture to rest for 10 minutes. Add the coconut meat to the marinade and mix it around so it gets completely coated with the marinade. Remove as much air as possible from the bag, seal, and place it in the refrigerator for 8 to 24 hours. During the marinating time, remove the bag from the refrigerator and work the coconut meat around so the marinade is fully incorporated into it. Remove the coconut from the marinade and arrange in a single layer in your choice of dryer. Dry at 135°F as directed on pages 16–19.

Cheesy Cauliflower Jerky

Sometimes you just want a snack you can eat by the handful without feeling guilty, or at least I do.
While I'd love nothing more than to devour an entire bag of Cheetos some days, it's just not something my brain will let my mouth and stomach do. So, I make a big batch of this cheesy cauliflower. Does it taste the same? No, but it's a close second and I think it's actually tastier because it tastes like more than just cheese. It's got tanginess from some mustard and lemon juice along with a little cayenne to keep things interesting. But with this recipe I can get in my daily vegetable serving and really enjoy it.

INGREDIENTS

¼ cup beer

3 tablespoons Cheddar cheese powder

2 teaspoons Dijon mustard

1 teaspoon sesame oil

1 teaspoon Tabasco sauce

1 teaspoon kosher salt

½ teaspoon liquid hickory smoke

½ teaspoon lemon juice

1 (2-pound) head of cauliflower, cut into small, equal-size florets

INSTRUCTIONS

1. In a 1-gallon resealable plastic freezer bag, mix together all the ingredients, except the cauliflower, and let sit for 10 minutes. Add the florets to the marinade and mix so they all get well coated with the marinade. Remove from the marinade and arrange in a single layer in your choice of dryer. Dry at 135°F as directed on pages 16–19 for 4 to 6 hours.

Wasabi Tofu Jerky

Do you like sushi? How about that fantastic sticky rice that comes with your sushi or roll? If you like that, too, you're going to love this wasabi tofu jerky. It's a great flavor combination that's very familiar to all you sushi lovers because it tastes almost exactly like that sushi rice. But this version has more protein than carbs.

INGREDIENTS

- ¼ cup water
- ¼ cup soy sauce
- 2 tablespoons wasabi powder
- 1 tablespoon lemon juice
- 2 teaspoons sugar
- 2 teaspoons unseasoned rice vinegar
- 1 teaspoon grated fresh ginger
- 1 (12-ounce) package extra-firm tofu, cut into 24 strips

INSTRUCTIONS

1. In a 1-gallon resealable plastic freezer bag, thoroughly mix together all the ingredients, except the tofu, and allow the mixture to rest for 10 minutes. Add the tofu strips to the marinade and mix them around so they get completely coated with the marinade. Remove as much air as possible from the bag, seal, and place it in the refrigerator for 8 to 24 hours. During the marinating time, remove the bag from the refrigerator and carefully work the tofu around so the marinade is fully incorporated into it. Remove the strips from the marinade and arrange in a single layer in your choice of dryer. Dry at 115°F as directed on pages 16–19.

CHAPTER 8

For Your Pets

Don't forget your furry friends when you're making jerky . . . they like jerkied meats, too. However, you don't want to feed them the highly seasoned recipes that you're eating. Some of those ingredients may not be good for them. That's why I've included jerky recipes especially for them.

None of these recipes require any special ingredients or techniques on your part.

A few tips to make your furry friends jerky-making life easier:

- The ingredients you use for your pets' jerky should be as clean as possible; that is, pet treats should have as few ingredients as possible. You should treat their ingredients much as you treat your own ingredients.

- Buying bone-in, skin-on chicken breasts is a real money saver. Yes, a bit more work is involved because you need to bone and skin the chicken before slicing and drying. You can take those chicken breast bones and toss them into a big pot with water and some vegetables and make your own chicken stock. Then you can either give that to your four-legged friend, you can eat it or you can pour it into a container and freeze it for later use. You can also fry the skin for something that tastes better than bacon . . . but that's for another time.

- Slicing the sweet potatoes on a mandoline is the fastest and easiest way to get really even slices from something that's so hard. But a mandoline is also the fastest way to lose a chunk of your finger in the kitchen. Make sure you use the guard at all times when using a mandoline. (I'm speaking from experience.)

Hot Diggity Dog

Our furry friends like jerky, too, and it's so easy to make it for them, why would you buy packaged treats? While hot dogs aren't something you usually think of feeding to your pup, when you use all-natural, preservatives-free, low-sodium hot dogs, it's perfectly fine. You decide if you want to slice them into rounds or cut them into long strips.

INGREDIENTS

1 16-ounce package all-natural, preservatives-free, very low-sodium all-beef hot dogs

INSTRUCTIONS

1. Slice the hot dogs into ⅜-inch coins and/or lengthwise into three equally thick strips and arrange in a single layer in your choice of dryer. Dry as directed on pages 16–19. Pat with paper towels to absorb any excess oil and store in an airtight container in the refrigerator.

Sausage Doggie

I used a pork/beef combination sausage to make a batch of these for my friends' dog Sammie. All-natural, preservatives-free, low-sodium sausage is a perfectly healthy food for dogs to have as a treat. Apparently they were so popular that Sammie learned a few new tricks. It seems he would do anything to get more of these treats.

INGREDIENTS

1 16-ounce package, all-natural, preservatives-free, very low-sodium sausage

INSTRUCTIONS

1. Slice the sausages into ⅜-inch coins and/or lengthwise into equally thick strips and arrange in a single layer in your choice of dryer. Dry as directed on pages 16–19. Pat with paper towels to absorb any excess oil and store in an airtight container in the refrigerator.

Liver Snax

If you make dried liver jerky for your furry little friends, you will be the king/queen of their world. Of course, you will be paying for it in the awful smell it produces while drying, but rest assured, you will be very well rewarded. I recommend you dry this one out in your garage. Just sayin'.

INGREDIENTS

1 pound liver

INSTRUCTIONS

1. Slice the liver into equal-width strips and lay them on the fruit rollup tray of a dehydrator. Do not just lay them directly on the drying rack or you'll be picking pieces of liver off the plastic tray for weeks! (Been there, done that.) If you can, set the dehydrator in your garage or some other part of your house when you dry the liver. If I told you it smelled pretty bad while it was drying, you'd hate me for not being more direct. *It stinks!* But just remember how much your dog will love you for it. Dry as directed on pages 16–19.

Sweet Potato Dog Treats

While my dog wouldn't let anything pass her lips that wasn't first walking this planet, most dogs that I know *love* dried sweet potato treats. They're so easy and inexpensive to make, why wouldn't you just bake up a tray of them for your best furry friend? Plus, they are full of vitamins and nutrients that are as good for your pet as they are for you.

INGREDIENTS

1 large sweet potato

INSTRUCTIONS

1. Slice the sweet potato thinly (about ³⁄₁₆-inch thick) on a mandoline, either into coins or long strips. Arrange in a single layer in your choice of dryer. If you are drying in the oven, lay the sweet potato in a single layer on top of a cooling rack that has been set in a rimmed baking sheet. This will allow the air to circulate all around the potato slices and keep them from sticking to the pan. Dry at 145°F as directed on pages 16–19.

Chicken Treats For Your Furry Friend

I started making dehydrated chicken breast treats for my dog a long time ago. Once I realized that I could make them more cheaply than I could buy them, it was homemade all the way. Then I started hearing all those news reports about dogs getting sick from imported chicken treats and I kept on making my own. We did a little taste test with her and she took the homemade treat every time. While it seems as if dogs will eat anything (hello? shoes?), they can tell the difference . . . and it matters.

INGREDIENTS

4 to 5 pounds boneless, skinless chicken breast slabs

INSTRUCTIONS

1. Arrange the chicken in a single layer in your choice of dehydrator. Dry as directed on pages 16–19.

Parting Thoughts

I hope you've enjoyed this book as much as I enjoyed writing it and creating the recipes. It really was a lot of fun. It got me through a major move, it helped me make a lot of new friends (no one will turn down the offer of jerky . . . and they will keep coming back for more), it opened new doors for me, it introduced me to lots of new people, and I learned a few things along the way.

ACKNOWLEDGMENTS

I want to thank all of my taste testers for their perseverance
and honesty. While all of these recipes have been tested
and tasted and passed judgment . . . food is very subjective.
Some of these jerkies you may love and some of them
you might not; feel free to change the recipes
and have fun with them.

Almost all of the ingredients used in this book are
available at your local grocery store. If you are not able to find
them there, you can easily find them on the Internet.
ENJOY!!!